LIVING WITH PURPOSE

Virtues That Shape Our Lives

Michael D Cress

TABLE OF CONTENTS

DEDICATION:

For my family, the pillars of my life, whose unwavering love and support have guided me through life. Your strength, wisdom, and kindness inspire me every day. This book is a testament to the foundation you've provided and the dreams you've encouraged.

AUTHOR BIO

In his capacity as Chairman and Managing Partner of MD Cress Ventures, Michael Cress is a key figure in shaping the strategic direction of the company and encouraging creative expansion. As such, Michael is committed to leading the organization toward innovative breakthroughs and long-term prosperity. Because he actively serves on the boards of numerous public and private firms, his experience goes beyond his principal work at MD Cress Ventures. Michael's influence extends to the philanthropic sector as well, as he contributes his leadership to a number of charities and charity organizations, demonstrating his dedication to improving society. Michael lives in Austin, Texas, where he continues to strike a balance between his work and his community service.

PROLOGUE

What if it's not about where we end up? What if it's about who we become on the way there?

In a world that often feels overwhelmed by noise, haste, and uncertainty, there exists a quiet but potent force in the simple acts of seeking and sharing positivity. It's within the gentle embrace of a kind word, the warmth of a genuine smile, and the strength of a hopeful thought that we find the truest essence of our humanity. This book is a collection of such moments—tiny sparks of light that have the power to pierce through even the darkest times in our lives.

In our fast-paced, often chaotic lives, it's easy to forget the impact that positivity can have on our well-being and the lives of those around us. We may find ourselves caught up in the rush of daily routines, facing challenges that seem insurmountable, or feeling lost in the noise of the world. But within each of us lies the capacity to create change, to uplift, and to bring warmth into the lives of others. This book serves as a testament to that potential, a reminder that no matter how tough the journey, there is always a reason to hope, to dream, and to believe in the inherent goodness of life.

The quotes and stories within these pages are not merely words but are echoes of wisdom passed down through generations. They are the distilled thoughts and experiences of those who have faced life's greatest trials and emerged with a deeper understanding of what it means to live a life filled with purpose and joy. Each page is infused with the spirit of those who have found light even in the darkest times and have chosen to share that light with others.

This book is not just a collection of words—it is a reservoir of encouragement, a source of inspiration, and a gentle guide for the journey of life. It is intended for those moments when doubt begins to creep in, when the path forward seems unclear, or when the heart simply needs a reminder that kindness, love, and positivity are always within reach. In a world that can sometimes seem devoid of these qualities, this stands as a reminder that they are never truly lost, only waiting to be rediscovered.

Life is filled with challenges, moments of uncertainty, and times when the way ahead seems shrouded in darkness. Yet, it is also filled with opportunities to bring light into those very moments, to turn despair into hope, and to transform obstacles into stepping stones. The words within this book are meant to be a source of comfort during those difficult times, a reminder that you are never alone on your journey and that even the smallest acts of kindness can have a profound impact on the world around you.

The power of positivity lies not only in grand gestures but also in the small, everyday actions that often go unnoticed. A smile to a stranger, a word of encouragement to a friend, or a simple act of kindness can ripple outwards, creating a wave of positive energy that touches more lives than we may ever know. These words celebrate those moments, acknowledging their significance and encouraging us all to recognize the impact we can have.

We live in a world that often emphasizes the negative, the divisive, and the destructive. But within each of us lies the potential to counteract that negativity with positivity, to bring people together, and to create something beautiful out of the challenges we face. The reflections and quotes in this book are a testament to that potential, a reminder that no matter how small an action may seem, it can have a lasting and meaningful impact.

As you explore the pages of this book, take time to reflect on the words and the feelings they evoke. Let them inspire you to embrace positivity in your own life and to share it with others. Whether you are facing a difficult decision, navigating a challenging situation, or simply seeking a moment of peace, may you find the guidance, encouragement, and inspiration you need.

In the end, life is about the connections we make, the love we share, and the positive impact we leave behind. This book is a celebration of those connections, a tribute to the power of love and kindness, and a reminder that even in a world filled with noise, haste, and uncertainty, there is always room for positivity.

Remember that within you lies the power to make a difference, to be a source of strength in someone else's life, and to create a world filled with more compassion, understanding, and love. Welcome to a discussion of positivity—a journey that begins with a single step, a single word, and a single act of kindness. One that not only seeks to inspire but also to remind you of the power you hold within to change the world, one positive action at a time.

CHAPTER 1
INSPIRATION

"What lies behind us and what lies before us are tiny matters compared to what lies within us." — Ralph Waldo Emerson

Inspiration: The Driving Force Behind Human Potential

Life is a journey filled with peaks and valleys, moments of triumph, and times of challenge. Along this path, we often find ourselves seeking a source of strength, a spark to ignite our inner fire and guide us forward. Inspiration, like a gentle breeze or a roaring wave, has the power to uplift our spirits, renew our courage, and remind us of the limitless potential that lies within us all.

Inspiration is the spark that ignites our imagination, drives our ambitions, and fuels our creativity. It is a force that propels us beyond the ordinary, lifting us to new heights and encouraging us to reach for goals that once seemed unattainable. This powerful, often intangible feeling is the wellspring of our most profound ideas, actions, and achievements. It can be found in the quiet moments of reflection, the awe-inspiring wonders of nature, or the extraordinary stories of human perseverance and triumph.

At its core, inspiration is about connection—connecting with our innermost desires, dreams, and potentials. It is the moment when our inner vision aligns with the external world, creating a sense of clarity and purpose. Inspiration often strikes unexpectedly, revealing new possibilities and perspectives that were previously obscured. It can be triggered by a myriad of sources: a moving piece of art, an uplifting conversation, a personal challenge, or a simple act of kindness.

Inspiration's ability to transform our outlook on life is one of its most remarkable qualities. When we are inspired, we see the world through a different lens, where obstacles become opportunities and failures become stepping stones. This shift in perspective enables us to envision new paths and possibilities, encouraging us to take bold steps toward our goals. Inspiration infuses our actions with energy and enthusiasm, making the journey toward our aspirations not just achievable but also deeply fulfilling.

Inspiration and Creativity

Inspiration is a catalyst for creativity. It acts as a muse, awakening our imaginative faculties and enabling us to think outside the box. Creative breakthroughs often arise from moments of inspiration when our minds are free to explore uncharted territories and innovative ideas. Whether in the arts, sciences, or everyday problem-solving, inspiration drives us to push boundaries and explore new frontiers. It encourages experimentation and exploration, leading to discoveries and advancements that can have a profound impact on our lives and the world.

The relationship between inspiration and creativity is symbiotic. While inspiration can spark creativity, creativity often nurtures and sustains inspiration. Engaging in creative activities can lead to new insights and ideas, which in turn can inspire further exploration and innovation. This dynamic interplay between inspiration and creativity is essential for personal growth and the advancement of human knowledge.

Inspiration as a Source of Influence

Moreover, inspiration has the power to influence and uplift others. When we share our sources of inspiration—whether through storytelling, mentorship, or simply by living our truth—we can inspire those around us to pursue their own passions and dreams. Inspirational figures often serve as role models, demonstrating what is possible through their actions and achievements. Their stories of overcoming adversity, achieving greatness, and making a positive impact serve as symbols of hope and motivation for others.

Sharing inspiration with others can create a reverberating impact, where one person's journey of triumph and perseverance encourages others to embark on their own paths of self-discovery and growth. By leading by example and offering support, we contribute to a culture of inspiration that can uplift entire communities and drive collective progress.

The Evolving Nature of Inspiration

Inspiration is not a static experience but a dynamic process that evolves over time. It requires openness and receptivity, as well as a willingness to embrace change and growth. To stay inspired, we must continually seek out new experiences, challenge our assumptions, and remain curious about the world. This ongoing journey of discovery and self-improvement ensures that inspiration remains a vibrant and integral part of our lives.

Maintaining inspiration involves cultivating habits and practices that foster creativity and personal growth. Engaging in activities that stimulate the mind, such as reading, exploring new interests, and connecting with others, can help keep the spark of inspiration alive. Additionally, being open to new experiences and perspectives can provide fresh sources of inspiration and keep our creative energies flowing.

Navigating Periods of Lack of Inspiration

While inspiration is a powerful force, it is also important to recognize that it is not always constant. There will be times when we feel uninspired or disconnected from our creative wellspring. During these periods, it is crucial to cultivate patience and perseverance. Inspiration often returns when we least expect it and maintaining a routine of exploration and reflection can help rekindle the spark when it seems to wane. Embracing these ebbs and flows as a natural part of the creative process can help us navigate periods of stagnation and reawaken our passion.

Periods of lack of inspiration can be challenging, but they also offer opportunities for growth and reflection. During these times, it can be helpful to revisit past sources of inspiration, engage in self-care practices, and explore new avenues for creative expression. By acknowledging and accepting these moments, we can create space for inspiration to reemerge and continue guiding us on our journey.

Finding Inspiration in Everyday Moments

Inspiration can also be found in the everyday moments of life. It is not always about grand achievements or monumental shifts; sometimes, it is the small, seemingly insignificant experiences that can provide the most profound insights. Finding beauty in the ordinary, appreciating the simple joys, and recognizing the value in small acts of kindness can all serve as sources of inspiration. By remaining attuned to these moments, we can maintain a sense of wonder and gratitude that fuels our creativity and motivation.

Everyday moments offer opportunities for inspiration that are often overlooked. Simple activities such as observing nature, spending time with loved ones, or engaging in acts of kindness can provide valuable insights and renew our sense of purpose. By cultivating mindfulness and being present in these moments, we can draw inspiration from the richness of everyday life.

The Personal Nature of Inspiration

Ultimately, inspiration is a deeply personal and unique experience. What inspires one person may differ vastly from what inspires another, and that diversity is a testament to the richness of the human experience. It is through exploring our own sources of inspiration and understanding what resonates with us that we can cultivate a more fulfilling and purposeful life. Whether it is through art, nature, relationships, or personal challenges, inspiration is a vital force that drives us to strive for greatness and to live authentically.

Understanding our personal sources of inspiration involves introspection and self-awareness. By reflecting on what motivates and excites us, we can align our goals and actions with our true passions and values. This self-discovery process is essential for creating a life that is meaningful and fulfilling, and it allows us to harness the power of inspiration in a way that is uniquely our own.

A Tribute to the Indomitable Human Spirit

This collection of thoughts is a testament to the indomitable human spirit—a spirit that refuses to be diminished by hardship, that rises above adversity, and that constantly strives for greatness. These words, spoken by thinkers, dreamers, and doers from across time and space, are more than just phrases on a page. They are the echoes of countless voices that have faced the same doubts, fears, and hopes that we encounter today.

In these pages, you will find stories and quotes of those who have dared to dream big, the encouragement of those who have overcome the odds, and the guidance of those who have walked the path before us. A reminder that no matter how dark the night, there is always a dawn.

The Role of Inspirational Words in Our Lives

Inspirational words can serve as powerful reminders of our potential and resilience. They encapsulate profound truths and insights in a concise and impactful manner, offering guidance and motivation during challenging times. By reflecting, we can gain new perspectives, renew our commitment to our goals, and find the strength to persevere in the face of adversity.

Quotes from inspirational figures can also provide comfort and encouragement, helping us to navigate our own journeys with greater confidence and clarity. They offer a sense of connection to those who have faced similar struggles and achieved remarkable successes, reminding us that we are not alone in our endeavors.

There will be days when your resolve is tested, when your goals seem out of reach, and when you need a reminder that you are capable of achieving more than you ever imagined. Let these words inspire you to take that next step, to push through the obstacles, and to believe in the power of your dreams.

As you continue your journey, may you find the motivation you need to pursue your passions, the strength to face your challenges, and the inspiration to become the best version of yourself. This is your path, and within you lies the power to shape it into something extraordinary.

The Boundless Nature of Inspiration

Welcome to a world where inspiration knows no bounds. Inspiration is a force that transcends limits and boundaries, offering us the potential to achieve greatness and live authentically. It is a reminder that within each of us lies the power to create, to innovate, and to overcome. By embracing the boundless nature of inspiration, we open ourselves to new possibilities and experiences that can transform our lives and the world around us.

Inspiration is not a finite resource but a dynamic and ever-renewing force. By remaining open to its influence and actively seeking out sources of inspiration, we can continually fuel our creativity and drive. Whether through personal experiences, the wisdom of others, or the beauty of the world, inspiration is a constant companion on our journey toward self-discovery and achievement.

Inspiration is a vital force that drives us to strive for greatness, to embrace new opportunities, and to live authentically. It is the spark that ignites our imagination, fuels our creativity, and transforms our outlook on life. Through inspiration, we connect with our innermost desires and potentials, enabling us to overcome challenges and achieve our goals.

CHAPTER 2
KINDNESS

Compassion is the greatest form of love that humans have to offer. I have this theory that if one person can go out of their way to show compassion, then it will start a chain reaction of the same. People will never know how far a little kindness can go."
— Rachel Joy Scott

A Transformative Power: A Journey into Kindness

Conversations can sometimes feel harsh and unforgiving, but kindness is the gentle force that softens our edges, bridges our differences and brings warmth to our hearts. It is the simple yet profound acts of kindness—both given and received—that remind us of our shared humanity and the deep connections that bind us together. This collection celebrates kindness in all its forms. From the quiet gestures that go unnoticed to the grand acts that change lives, these words reflect the beauty and power of compassion. They remind us that kindness is not just an action but a way of being—a choice we make each day to bring a little more light into the world.

Kindness is the language of the heart, understood by all, and needed by all. It has the ability to heal wounds, lift spirits, and create ripples that extend far beyond the moment. In these pages, you will find the wisdom of those who have recognized the transformative power of kindness, who have made it their mission to spread love, and who understand that even the smallest acts can have the greatest impact.

At its core, kindness is an expression of empathy. It involves recognizing and responding to the feelings and needs of others with genuine care and consideration. When we extend kindness, we are essentially putting ourselves in another's shoes, offering support, comfort, and compassion. This act of understanding fosters a sense of belonging and reinforces our shared humanity. It allows us to transcend our differences and connect on a deeper level, creating a sense of unity and mutual respect.

The Ripple Effect of Kindness

One of the most powerful aspects of kindness is its ability to create positive ripple effects. A single act of kindness can have far-reaching consequences, inspiring others to pay it forward and perpetuating a cycle of generosity and compassion. This effect can transform communities and societies, fostering environments where people feel valued and supported. For example, a simple gesture like holding the door open for someone, offering a compliment, or lending a helping hand can spark a chain reaction of goodwill and cooperation.

The ripple effect of kindness is not limited to immediate actions. It can extend far beyond the initial act, influencing others in ways that may not be immediately visible. For instance, a kind word or gesture can inspire someone to act with kindness in their own lives, creating a domino effect that spreads throughout a community. This phenomenon illustrates the interconnectedness of our actions and the profound impact that kindness can have on the world around us.

The Benefits of Kindness for the Giver and the Receiver

Kindness also has significant benefits for both the giver and the receiver. Research has shown that engaging in acts of kindness can enhance mental and emotional well-being, reducing stress, anxiety, and depression. When we help others, we experience a sense of purpose and fulfillment, which can improve our overall mood and quality of life. This reciprocal nature of kindness means that both the giver and the receiver gain from the interaction, reinforcing the idea that kindness is a mutual exchange of positive energy.

For the giver, acts of kindness can boost self-esteem, foster a sense of connection, and provide a meaningful way to contribute to the well-being of others. The act of giving, whether through time, resources, or simply a kind word, creates a sense of satisfaction and joy that can have lasting effects on one's mental and emotional health. This positive feedback loop encourages individuals to continue practicing kindness, creating a cycle of generosity and compassion.

For the receiver, the impact of kindness can be profound. Acts of kindness can provide comfort during difficult times, offer reassurance and support, and restore faith in the goodness of humanity. The experience of receiving kindness can also inspire individuals to pass on the kindness they have received, further perpetuating the ripple effect of positive energy and goodwill.

Kindness and Community Impact

In addition to its emotional benefits, kindness can have tangible impacts on individuals and communities. Acts of kindness can address immediate needs, alleviate suffering, and contribute to a more just and equitable society. For instance, community-driven initiatives, such as food drives, mentorship programs, and support networks, are examples of how kindness can be harnessed to address social issues and improve the quality of life for those in need. By working together with a spirit of kindness, we can tackle systemic challenges and create lasting positive change.

Communities that prioritize kindness tend to have stronger social bonds, lower levels of conflict, and a greater sense of collective well-being. When kindness is embedded in the fabric of a community, it fosters a culture of mutual support and cooperation, where individuals feel valued and connected. This sense of community can lead to increased civic engagement, social cohesion, and a more resilient society that is better equipped to address challenges and adapt to change.

The Challenges of Practicing Kindness

Despite its many benefits, kindness is not always easy to practice. It requires us to be mindful and intentional in our interactions, to set aside our own judgments and biases, and to approach others with an open heart. It involves a conscious effort to understand and address the needs of others, even when it may be inconvenient or challenging. Practicing kindness means choosing compassion over indifference, understanding over judgment, and support over neglect.

One of the challenges of practicing kindness is navigating the complexities of human relationships. Kindness does not always come naturally, especially in situations where we may feel hurt, frustrated, or overwhelmed. It requires a level of emotional maturity and self-awareness to respond with kindness, even in difficult circumstances. This challenge is compounded by the fast-paced, often stressful nature of modern life, which can make it difficult to slow down and be present in our interactions with others.

Kindness and Personal Growth

The practice of kindness also demands self-awareness and personal growth. It involves reflecting on our own behaviors, recognizing areas where we can improve, and striving to align our actions with our values. Kindness is a lifelong journey of developing empathy, building relationships, and contributing to the well-being of others. It requires us to continually assess and refine our approach, to learn from our experiences, and to remain committed to fostering a culture of compassion.

Engaging in acts of kindness can also lead to personal growth by challenging us to step outside of our comfort zones and consider the needs of others. It encourages us to develop greater empathy and understanding, which can enhance our relationships and deepen our connection to the world around us. Through the practice of kindness, we can cultivate a more compassionate and inclusive perspective, which in turn contributes to our own personal development and sense of fulfillment.

Kindness as a Collective Ethos

Moreover, kindness is not just about individual actions but about creating a collective ethos of compassion. In families, workplaces, schools, and communities, fostering a culture of kindness involves encouraging and supporting one another, celebrating acts of generosity, and addressing conflicts with empathy and understanding. By cultivating an environment where kindness is valued and practiced, we can create a more harmonious and supportive society.

Creating a culture of kindness requires collective effort and a commitment to prioritizing compassion in all aspects of life. This involves recognizing and celebrating acts of kindness, providing opportunities for individuals to engage in meaningful contributions, and addressing challenges with empathy and understanding. By working together to foster a culture of kindness, we can create a more inclusive, empathetic, and just society.

The Role of Kindness in Social Change

As we reflect on the nature and impact of kindness, we are reminded of its profound significance in our lives and the world around us. Kindness is a testament to our capacity for love, understanding, and connection. It is a reminder that, despite the challenges and complexities of life, there is always room for compassion and positivity. By embracing kindness as a fundamental aspect of our interactions, we can contribute to a more inclusive, empathetic, and just world.

Kindness also plays a critical role in driving social change. Acts of kindness, whether small or large, have the power to challenge injustice, promote equality, and inspire others to take action. Social movements throughout history have often been fueled by the collective kindness and compassion of individuals who recognize the need for change and are willing to work toward a better future.

Kindness and the Human Experience

This conversation is for those who believe in the goodness of people who seek to make the world a better place, one kind act at a time. It is a source of inspiration for when you need a reminder that kindness matters, and that your own kindness has the power to change lives, starting with your own.

Kindness is an integral part of the human experience, and its impact is felt in every aspect of our lives. From the simple interactions we have with strangers to the deep connections we share with loved ones, kindness is the thread that weaves together the fabric of our existence. It is through acts of kindness that we express our shared humanity, connect with others on a deeper level, and contribute to the well-being of the world around us.

The Power of Words in Spreading Kindness

As you read these thoughts, may they inspire you to carry kindness with you, to offer it freely, and to remember that in every interaction, you have the power to make a difference. Let these words help guide you toward a life filled with compassion, empathy, and love.

Words have the power to inspire, uplift, and encourage acts of kindness. This collection serves as a reminder of the importance of kindness in our lives and the impact it can have on the world. By reflecting on these words and incorporating their messages into our daily lives, we can create a more compassionate and connected world.

The Journey of Kindness

Welcome to a journey of kindness, where every word is a step toward a more compassionate world. Welcome to a collection that celebrates the best in us all.

The journey of kindness is a lifelong pursuit, one that requires continuous effort and commitment. It is a journey that challenges us to look beyond ourselves, to recognize the needs of others, and to act with compassion and generosity. This journey is not always easy, but it is one that is deeply rewarding and fulfilling.

Throughout this journey, we are reminded of the importance of kindness in all aspects of our lives. Whether in our personal relationships, our interactions with strangers, or our efforts to create positive change in the world, kindness is the force that drives us to be our best selves and to make a difference in the lives of others.

Kindness as a Universal Language

Kindness is a universal language, one that transcends cultural, linguistic, and geographical boundaries. It is a language that is understood and appreciated by all, regardless of background or beliefs. Acts of kindness have the power to bridge divides, foster understanding, and create connections between people from all walks of life.

In a world that is often divided by differences, kindness is the common thread that unites us. It reminds us of our shared humanity and our collective responsibility to care for one another. By embracing kindness as a universal language, we can create a more inclusive and compassionate world, one where everyone is valued and respected.

Kindness and Personal Transformation

The practice of kindness has the power to transform not only the lives of others but also our own lives. When we make kindness a priority, we begin to see the world in a different light. We become more attuned to the needs of others, more empathetic in our interactions, and more committed to making a positive impact in the world.

Personal transformation through kindness involves a shift in perspective, one that prioritizes compassion and understanding over judgment and indifference. It requires us to be mindful of our actions and to recognize the power we have to make a difference in the lives of others. By embracing kindness as a way of life, we can create a wave of positivity that extends far beyond ourselves.

The Role of Kindness in Building a Better Future

As we look to the future, kindness will continue to play a crucial role in building a better world. In the face of global challenges, such as inequality, environmental degradation, and social injustice, kindness offers a path forward. It is through acts of kindness, both large and small that we can address these challenges and create a more just and equitable society.

Kindness is not just a passive virtue but an active force for good. It requires us to take action, to stand up for what is right, and to work toward a better future for all. By embracing kindness as a guiding principle, we can contribute to the creation of a world that is more compassionate, inclusive, and just.

A Story of Kindness: Rachel Joy Scott

Rachel Joy Scott was a compassionate and vibrant student at Columbine High School in Littleton, Colorado. Known for her kindness and faith, Rachel made it her mission to reach out to those who felt isolated or marginalized. She believed in the power of small acts of kindness, understanding that even the simplest gestures could have a profound impact on someone's life. Rachel often went out of her way to connect with her peers, offering a kind word, a smile, or a listening ear to those who needed it most. She embodied the belief that every person mattered and that everyone deserved to feel seen and valued.

On April 20, 1999, Rachel's life was tragically cut short when she became the first victim of the Columbine High School massacre, a devastating event that shocked the nation and left an indelible mark on the community. Rachel was the same age as my daughter, just 17 years old. I went from the daily routine children left for school in the morning to suddenly fearing for their safety. The world had changed in an instant.

In the days following her death, Rachel's father discovered her journals, which were filled with her thoughts on love, faith, and kindness. These writings revealed the depth of her compassion and her unwavering belief in the importance of caring for others. She wrote about her desire to make a difference in the world, hoping that her small acts of kindness would inspire others to do the same.

Rachel's life and legacy inspired the creation of "Rachel's Challenge," a nationwide movement dedicated to promoting kindness, compassion, and empathy in schools. The program encourages students to create a culture of understanding and support, challenging them to reach out to those who feel alone and to make a positive impact in their communities. Through "Rachel's Challenge," her message of love and kindness continues to resonate, reminding people that even one person can make a significant difference. I was honored when Rachel's father, Darrell Scott, asked me to serve on the organization's board of directors, a role I continue to hold with pride today.

Rachel Joy Scott's story is a powerful testament to the enduring impact of kindness. Her life, though tragically short, continues to inspire millions to embrace empathy, understanding, and the belief that every small act of kindness has the potential to change the world.

Embracing the Power of Kindness

Kindness is a powerful force that has the ability to transform lives, create connections, and build a better world. It is a universal language that transcends boundaries and unites us in our shared humanity. Through acts of kindness, we express our empathy, compassion, and love for others, contributing to a more harmonious and supportive society.

As we navigate the journey of life, let us remember the importance of kindness in all that we do. Let us strive to be kind to ourselves, to others, and to the world around us. By making kindness a priority, we can create a cascading impact of positivity that extends far beyond ourselves, touching the lives of others and making the world a better place for all.

This collection of thoughts is a celebration of the transformative power of kindness. It serves as a reminder that kindness is not just an action but a way of being—a choice we make each day to bring a little more light into the world.

CHAPTER 3
FRIENDSHIP

"Friends are the family you choose." — Jess C. Scott

Friendship: The Cherished Bond That Shapes Our Lives

Friendship is one of the most cherished and enduring bonds we form in our lives. It transcends the mere act of knowing someone and delves into the realms of trust, loyalty, and mutual respect. Friends are the chosen family we surround ourselves with, the people who stand by us through life's ups and downs, who share in our joys, and provide comfort in our sorrows. This unique relationship plays an integral role in shaping who we are, offering us a sense of belonging and understanding that is often unparalleled.

The Foundation of Trust in Friendship

At the heart of every true friendship is trust. Trust is the foundation upon which friendships are built, and it is this trust that allows us to be vulnerable with one another. In a world where we are often expected to wear masks and present our best selves, friendship offers a safe space where we can be our authentic selves. We share our dreams, fears, and insecurities, knowing that our friends will hold these confidences with care and without judgment. This deep level of trust fosters a connection that goes beyond the superficial, creating bonds that can withstand the test of time.

Trust in friendship is not just about keeping secrets or being honest with one another; it is about having faith in each other's intentions and actions. It is about knowing that your friend will be there for you, not just in the good times but also when life is challenging. This trust is built over time, through shared experiences, and it deepens as friends consistently show up for each other, proving their reliability and commitment.

Loyalty: The Unwavering Support of Friendship

Loyalty is another cornerstone of friendship. A loyal friend is someone who remains steadfast in their support, even when the world seems to turn against you. They are there in times of need, offering a shoulder to cry on, a listening ear, or simply their presence. This loyalty is not just about being there in the tough times; it also means celebrating your successes, standing by your side during moments of triumph, and genuinely sharing in your happiness. Loyalty in friendship is a mutual exchange; it's about being there for each other, no matter the circumstances, and knowing that you can rely on each other without hesitation.

Loyalty in friendship is often tested in difficult situations. There may be moments when misunderstandings arise or when circumstances create distance between friends. However, true loyalty means weathering these storms together, finding ways to overcome challenges, and reaffirming the bond that exists. This unwavering support is what makes friendship so unique and irreplaceable. It is a commitment to being there for each other through thick and thin, and it is this loyalty that often defines the strength of a friendship.

The Joy and Simplicity of Friendship

The beauty of friendship lies in its simplicity and the joy it brings to our lives. Friends are the people with whom we share our everyday moments, the mundane as well as the extraordinary. Whether it's a quick chat over coffee, a late-night conversation, or a spontaneous adventure, these shared experiences create memories that enrich our lives. Friends are the ones who know our quirks, understand our sense of humor, and accept us for who we are. In their company, we find laughter, comfort, and a sense of belonging that is deeply fulfilling.

The joy of friendship is often found in the little things, inside jokes, shared hobbies, and the comfort of knowing someone understands you without the need for explanation. These simple pleasures form the fabric of our daily lives and create a sense of continuity and stability. Friendships bring color and vibrancy to our existence, providing moments of joy that brighten even the darkest days.

Friendship and Personal Growth

Friendship also plays a significant role in our personal growth. Our friends often challenge us to see the world from different perspectives, encouraging us to step out of our comfort zones and embrace new experiences. They are the ones who push us to be better versions of ourselves, offering constructive criticism when needed and cheering us on as we strive to achieve our goals. Through their support and encouragement, we find the strength to overcome obstacles and the confidence to pursue our dreams.

Friendships can act as a mirror, reflecting back to us our strengths and weaknesses. They provide us with honest feedback and help us to see ourselves more clearly. In the process of growing together, friends also grow individually, learning from each other and evolving in ways that might not have been possible alone. This mutual growth is one of the most rewarding aspects of friendship, as it allows both individuals to reach new heights and explore new dimensions of their personalities.

The Effort Required to Maintain Friendships

However, like any relationship, friendship requires effort and nurturing to thrive. It is not immune to misunderstandings, conflicts, or the pressures of time and distance. Maintaining a strong friendship involves communication, empathy, and a willingness to work through challenges together. Open and honest communication is key to resolving conflicts and ensuring that both parties feel heard and understood. Empathy allows us to put ourselves in our friend's shoes, to understand their feelings, and to respond with kindness and compassion.

Effective communication in friendship means being willing to discuss difficult topics, to listen actively, and to express ourselves openly. It means being vulnerable, sharing our true thoughts and feelings, and trusting that our friends will respond with understanding. This level of communication helps to prevent misunderstandings and to resolve conflicts before they become larger issues.

Empathy in friendship is about being there for each other, not just physically, but emotionally. It means being attuned to your friend's needs and feelings, offering support when they are struggling, and celebrating with them when they are happy. This mutual empathy deepens the connection between friends and fosters a sense of closeness and intimacy that is essential for a lasting friendship.

The Challenge of Distance in Friendship

Distance, whether physical or emotional, can be a test of friendship. Life often takes us in different directions, and it can be challenging to maintain the same level of closeness when circumstances change. However, true friendship has a way of enduring these tests. While the frequency of interaction may decrease, the bond remains strong, sustained by the trust, loyalty, and shared history that define the relationship. Reconnecting with a friend after a long time apart often feels like no time has passed at all, a testament to the deep connection that underlies the friendship.

Maintaining a long-distance friendship requires intentional effort. It involves staying connected through phone calls, messages, and visits when possible. It also means being understanding of each other's lives and schedules, recognizing that the bond of friendship can endure even when physical proximity is not possible. The ability to maintain a strong friendship across distance is a testament to the depth of the relationship and the commitment of both individuals.

Emotional Support in Friendship

Friendship is also a source of immense emotional support. In times of crisis, our friends are often the first people we turn to. They offer comfort, reassurance, and a sense of stability when everything else feels uncertain. This emotional support is reciprocal; just as we lean on our friends, they also rely on us in their times of need. This mutual support strengthens the bond of friendship, creating a sense of interdependence that enhances the connection.

Emotional support in friendship is about being present for each other in both good times and bad. It means being willing to listen without judgment, to offer advice when asked, and to provide comfort when needed. This support is not just about solving problems but about being there, offering a sense of companionship and solidarity that can make even the most difficult situations feel more manageable.

The reciprocal nature of emotional support in friendship means that both parties benefit from the relationship. By offering support to our friends, we strengthen the bond between us and create a foundation of trust and mutual respect. This mutual support is one of the most valuable aspects of friendship, as it provides both individuals with a sense of security and belonging.

The Evolution of Friendships Over Time

Moreover, friendships evolve over time. As we grow and change, so too do our friendships. The friends we make in childhood often see us through different stages of life, witnessing our growth and transformation. New friendships formed in adulthood are often based on shared values and interests, reflecting the person we have become. Each friendship, whether old or new, contributes to our lives in unique ways, offering us different perspectives and experiences that enrich our understanding of the world.

Friendships that last over time often deepen and become more meaningful as both individuals grow and change. These long-term friendships provide a sense of continuity and history, as both friends share a wealth of memories and experiences that create a strong bond. These friendships often feel like a constant in an ever-changing world, providing a sense of stability and connection that is deeply comforting.

New friendships, on the other hand, bring fresh perspectives and new experiences into our lives. They offer us the opportunity to connect with people who share our current interests and values, reflecting the person we have become. These new friendships can be just as meaningful as those that have lasted for years, offering us a chance to continue growing and evolving as individuals.

The Role of Friendship in Mental and Physical Health

Friendship is a vital part of the human experience, and its impact extends beyond emotional support and personal growth. Studies have shown that strong social connections, including friendships, are linked to better mental and physical health. People with close friendships tend to experience lower levels of stress, depression, and anxiety. They are also more likely to engage in healthy behaviors, such as regular exercise and a balanced diet, and they tend to have better overall well-being.

The mental health benefits of friendship are significant. Having someone to talk to, to share experiences with, and to rely on in times of need can greatly reduce feelings of loneliness and isolation. This sense of connection and belonging is crucial for mental health, as it helps to foster a positive outlook on life and provides a buffer against the challenges and stresses of everyday life.

Physical health is also positively impacted by friendship. Research has shown that people with strong social networks tend to live longer, have stronger immune systems, and recover more quickly from illness and surgery. The support and encouragement of friends can also motivate individuals to take better care of themselves, to make healthier choices, and to engage in activities that promote physical well-being.

The Challenges of Modern Friendship

While friendship offers many benefits, it also faces challenges in the modern world. The fast pace of life, the demands of work and family, and the increasing reliance on digital communication can make it difficult to maintain close and meaningful friendships. The rise of social media, while providing a platform for connection, can sometimes lead to superficial interactions that lack the depth and intimacy of face-to-face communication.

Maintaining friendships in the modern world requires intentional effort and a commitment to nurturing the relationship. It means making time for friends, even when life is busy, and prioritizing meaningful interactions over superficial connections. It also involves being mindful of the impact of digital communication on the quality of our friendships, and finding ways to maintain depth and intimacy in our interactions.

One way to overcome these challenges is to focus on quality over quantity in our friendships. Instead of trying to maintain a large number of superficial connections, we can focus on deepening the relationships that are most important to us. This might involve setting aside regular time to connect with friends, whether through phone calls, video chats, or in-person meetings. It also means being present and fully engaged in our interactions, rather than multitasking or allowing distractions to interfere.

The Role of Friendship in Times of Change

Friendship plays a crucial role during times of change and transition. Whether it is a move to a new city, a career change, or a major life event, friends provide the support and stability needed to navigate these changes. They offer a sense of continuity and familiarity, helping us to stay grounded even when everything around us is shifting.

During times of change, friends can also offer valuable perspective and advice. They can help us to see the situation from different angles, to weigh our options, and to make decisions with confidence. Their support and encouragement can provide the motivation needed to embrace change and to move forward with courage and resilience.

The importance of friendship during times of change is also reflected in the way that friends can help us to adapt and grow. They can introduce us to new experiences, help us to develop new skills, and encourage us to step out of our comfort zones. This support and encouragement are essential for personal growth and can help us to navigate change with greater ease and confidence.

Friendship and Cultural Differences

Friendship is a universal human experience, but it can take different forms in different cultures. Cultural differences in communication styles, social norms, and expectations can influence the way friendships are formed and maintained. Understanding and navigating these differences is important for building and sustaining cross-cultural friendships.

In some cultures, friendships are formed quickly and easily, with an emphasis on casual social interactions and a wide circle of acquaintances. In other cultures, friendships are formed more slowly and are based on deeper connections and shared values. These cultural differences can impact the way friendships are perceived and the level of intimacy and commitment involved.

Navigating cultural differences in friendship requires openness, understanding, and a willingness to learn from each other. It involves being mindful of different communication styles and social norms and finding ways to connect that are respectful of these differences. By embracing cultural diversity in our friendships, we can enrich our lives and gain a deeper understanding of the world.

Friendship Across Generations

Friendship is not limited to peers of the same age; it can also span across generations. Intergenerational friendships offer unique opportunities for learning, growth, and mutual support. These friendships can provide different perspectives and insights, helping individuals to bridge generational gaps and to build connections that transcend age.

Intergenerational friendships can be particularly valuable in providing a sense of continuity and connection to the past. Older friends can offer wisdom, guidance, and a broader perspective on life, while younger friends can bring energy, new ideas, and a fresh outlook. These relationships can be mutually beneficial, providing opportunities for learning and growth on both sides.

In families, intergenerational friendships often develop between grandparents and grandchildren, aunts and uncles and their nieces and nephews, or even between parents and their adult children. These friendships can provide a sense of family continuity and a connection to family history and traditions. They can also offer a source of support and companionship that is different from peer friendships, adding depth and richness to our social networks.

The Power of Friendship in Times of Adversity

The true strength of friendship often becomes evident in times of adversity. When life presents us with challenges, whether they are personal, professional, or health-related, friends are the ones who stand by us and offer their unwavering support. They provide a sense of stability and comfort, helping us to navigate difficult times with resilience and grace.

Friendship in times of adversity is not just about offering practical support; it is also about providing emotional support. True friends listen without judgment, offer a safe space to express emotions, and provide a sense of companionship that can make even the darkest moments feel less overwhelming. This support can be a lifeline, helping individuals to find the strength to keep going, even when the road ahead seems uncertain.

The power of friendship in adversity is also reflected in the way that friends can help us to find hope and meaning in difficult situations. They can help us to reframe challenges as opportunities for growth, to find silver linings in difficult circumstances, and to maintain a positive outlook even in the face of adversity. This support is invaluable, providing the encouragement and motivation needed to overcome challenges and to emerge stronger on the other side.

The Enduring Impact of Friendship

Friendship is a relationship that brings joy, comfort, and meaning to our lives. It is a bond that shapes who we are, offering us a sense of belonging, understanding, and support that is essential for our well-being. Friends are the people who walk alongside us on our journey, sharing in our triumphs, supporting us in our struggles, and simply being there through it all.

The enduring impact of friendship is seen in the way that these relationships continue to influence our lives, even after friends have come and gone. The memories, lessons, and experiences we share with our friends become a part of who we are, shaping our values, beliefs, and outlook on life. The bonds we form with our friends are among the most precious and enduring connections we have, and they play an essential role in shaping who we are.

In a world that is constantly changing, friendship remains a constant source of strength, love, and understanding. It is a reminder that we are not alone, that there are people who care for us, and that through these connections, we find a sense of belonging and purpose. The power of friendship is timeless, transcending the challenges of distance, time, and adversity and providing us with the support and companionship we need to navigate the complexities of life.

Celebrating the Gift of Friendship

Friendship is one of the most cherished and enduring bonds we form in our lives. It is a relationship built on trust, loyalty, and mutual respect, offering us a sense of belonging and understanding that is often unparalleled. Friends are the chosen family we surround ourselves with, the people who stand by us through life's ups and downs and who share in our joys and provide comfort in our sorrows.

At the heart of every true friendship is trust, which allows us to be vulnerable and authentic with one another. Loyalty in friendship is about unwavering support, standing by each other through thick and thin. The beauty of friendship lies in its simplicity and the joy it brings to our lives, enriching our existence with laughter, comfort, and shared experiences.

Friendship also plays a significant role in our personal growth, challenging us to see the world from different perspectives and encouraging us to step out of our comfort zones. Maintaining strong friendships requires effort, communication, and empathy, especially when distance and life changes test the bond. Emotional support in friendship is mutual, providing stability and reassurance in times of crisis.

Friendships evolve over time, contributing to our lives in unique ways and offering us different perspectives and experiences that enrich our understanding of the world. The impact of friendship extends beyond emotional support, positively influencing our mental and physical health, and offering a sense of belonging and connection that is crucial for our well-being.

In modern society, maintaining friendships can be challenging, but with intentional effort and a focus on quality interactions, these bonds can remain strong and meaningful. Friendship plays a crucial role during times of change, providing the support and stability needed to navigate transitions with resilience and grace. Cross-cultural and intergenerational friendships offer unique opportunities for learning and growth, enriching our lives with diverse perspectives and insights.

The power of friendship is especially evident in times of adversity, providing unwavering support and helping us to find hope and meaning in difficult situations. The enduring impact of friendship is seen in the way these relationships continue to influence our lives, shaping who we are and offering us a sense of belonging and purpose.

In conclusion, friendship is a vital part of the human experience, offering us joy, comfort, and meaning throughout our lives. It is a bond that shapes who we are and provides us with the support and companionship we need to navigate the complexities of life. The gift of friendship is timeless and enduring, a constant source of strength, love, and understanding that enriches our lives and brings us closer to our true selves. Let us celebrate and cherish the friendships in our lives, for they are among the most precious and enduring connections we have.

CHAPTER 4
COURAGE

**"Courage is not the absence of fear, but rather the judgment that something else is more important than fear."
— Ambrose Redmoon**

The Essence of Courage

In the tapestry of human experience, there is a thread that shines brighter than the rest, woven through the fabric of our fears and aspirations—courage. It is the quiet strength that propels us forward when the path is uncertain, the invisible force that steadies our hands and hearts in the face of adversity. Courage is not the absence of fear, but the mastery of it, the ability to walk boldly into the unknown despite trembling knees and a racing heart.

Throughout history, the greatest minds and souls have distilled the essence of courage into words that resonate through the ages, offering hope to those who falter. These are more than just words; they are the whispers of wisdom from those who have faced the storm and emerged stronger. They remind us that courage is not reserved for the extraordinary, but lies within each of us, waiting to be called upon in moments of trial and doubt.

Courage is found in the small, everyday acts of defiance against the darkness, in the choice to stand up when it would be easier to remain seated, to speak when silence is more comfortable, and to continue the journey when every muscle aches for rest. It is the lifeblood of heroes and the heartbeat of change. As you explore the following pages, let them ignite the spark of bravery within you, urging you to face your challenges with unwavering resolve, and to live each day with the courage to be your truest self.

Courage as a Fundamental Human Quality

Courage is a fundamental human quality that has been celebrated throughout history, from the tales of ancient heroes to the struggles of modern-day individuals. At its core, courage is the ability to confront fear, pain, danger, uncertainty, or intimidation, even when the odds seem insurmountable. It is the inner strength that drives us to face challenges head-on, to persevere in the face of adversity, and to stand up for what we believe in, even when it is difficult or unpopular.

One of the most significant aspects of courage is that it is not the absence of fear, but rather the determination to act despite it. Fear is a natural response to perceived threats or dangers, and it can be a powerful force that holds us back from pursuing our goals or standing up for our values. However, courage allows us to acknowledge our fears and move forward anyway, recognizing that some things are more important than the fear itself.

Courage in Everyday Life

Courage manifests in many forms, both big and small. For some, it may involve taking a stand against injustice or defending the rights of others, even when it comes at great personal risk. For others, courage might be found in everyday acts, such as speaking up in a difficult conversation, pursuing a dream despite doubts and setbacks, or simply continuing on in the face of life's challenges. Whether in grand gestures or quiet persistence, courage is what enables us to live authentically and to strive for our highest aspirations.

In personal growth, courage is essential. It pushes us out of our comfort zones and into the unknown, where real development occurs. It takes courage to confront our limitations, to admit when we are wrong, and to seek out new experiences that will expand our horizons. Without courage, we might remain stagnant, never daring to take the risks necessary for true growth and fulfillment.

The Role of Courage in Leadership

Courage is also a key element of leadership. Great leaders are often defined by their ability to make tough decisions in the face of uncertainty, to inspire others with their vision, and to remain steadfast in their principles despite external pressures. Leadership requires the courage to take responsibility, to navigate uncharted territories, and to make decisions that may not always be popular but are in the best interest of the greater good.

Leadership courage is particularly evident in times of crisis. When the path forward is unclear and the stakes are high, leaders must rely on their inner strength to guide their teams and communities through uncertainty. This may involve making difficult decisions, such as cutting budgets, laying off employees, or pivoting business strategies in response to changing circumstances. While these decisions may not be easy, they are often necessary for the survival and success of the organization or community.

Social Impact of Courage

Moreover, courage has a profound social impact. It is the driving force behind movements for change and progress. Throughout history, courageous individuals have stood up against oppression, fought for civil rights, and worked tirelessly to create a better world for future generations. These acts of bravery not only inspire others but also have the benefit of encouraging more people to take action and stand up for what is right.

The civil rights movement in the United States is a powerful example of the social impact of courage. Leaders like Martin Luther King Jr., Rosa Parks, and countless others demonstrated immense bravery in the face of systemic racism and violent opposition. Their courage to demand equality and justice inspired a nation and led to significant changes in laws and social attitudes. The courage of these individuals continues to inspire movements for social justice around the world, reminding us that change is possible when people are willing to stand up and fight for what is right.

Courage in Personal Development

In essence, courage is the quality that enables us to live fully and purposefully. It allows us to face life's inevitable challenges with resilience and grace. Courage is not always about heroic deeds or grand gestures; sometimes, it is found in the simple act of getting up each day and continuing on, even when the road is tough. It is the quiet resolve to keep moving forward, to keep trying, and to keep believing in ourselves and our dreams, no matter how difficult the journey may be.

In personal development, courage is the catalyst for growth and self-improvement. It takes courage to confront our weaknesses, to admit our mistakes, and to seek out new challenges that will push us beyond our current limitations. Whether it is learning a new skill, pursuing a passion, or making a major life change, courage is the driving force that propels us forward.

The Universality of Courage

Ultimately, courage is part of what makes us human. It is the inner flame that drives us to seek out the best in ourselves and in others, to strive for our dreams, and to stand firm in our convictions. It is through courage that we find our true strength and our greatest potential, and it is through courage that we can make a lasting impact on the world. The stories of courage, from ancient legends to contemporary heroes, remind us that the human spirit is capable of incredible feats when fueled by bravery. It is this courage that binds us together, inspires us to reach for more, and helps us navigate the complexities of life with hope and determination.

Courage is a universal quality, transcending cultures, languages, and borders. While the manifestations of courage may vary across different societies and historical periods, the underlying essence of courage remains the same—a willingness to face fear, to take risks, and to stand up for what is right. This universality of courage is what makes it such a powerful and enduring human quality.

Courage in Historical Contexts

Throughout history, courage has been celebrated and revered in various cultures and traditions. In ancient Greece, courage was one of the four cardinal virtues, along with wisdom, temperance, and justice. The Greek concept of courage, or *andreia*, was closely associated with the idea of facing danger and adversity with bravery and strength. This virtue was exemplified by the heroes of Greek mythology, such as Achilles and Hercules, who displayed extraordinary courage in their battles and quests.

In the context of medieval Europe, courage was a key component of the chivalric code that governed the behavior of knights. Chivalry emphasized the importance of bravery, honor, and loyalty, and knights were expected to demonstrate courage in both combat and in upholding the values of their society. This code of conduct was immortalized in the tales of King Arthur and the Knights of the Round Table, where courage was often portrayed as the defining characteristic of true heroism.

In many Indigenous cultures, courage is deeply intertwined with the values of community and respect for nature. Indigenous warriors were often revered for their bravery in protecting their people and their land, and courage was seen as a vital quality for leadership and survival. This understanding of courage was not limited to physical bravery but also included the courage to face spiritual challenges, to uphold traditions, and to stand up for the rights and dignity of the community.

Courage in Modern Society

In modern society, the concept of courage has evolved to encompass a broader range of experiences and challenges. While physical bravery is still celebrated, there is also a growing recognition of the importance of emotional and moral courage.

Emotional courage involves the willingness to be vulnerable, to express our true feelings, and to connect with others on a deep and authentic level. Moral courage, on the other hand, involves standing up for our values and principles, even when it is difficult or unpopular.

One of the most compelling examples of modern courage is found in the stories of individuals who have spoken out against injustice, often at great personal risk. Whistleblowers, for example, demonstrate moral courage by exposing corruption, fraud, or unethical practices within organizations, despite the potential consequences for their careers and personal lives. Their actions serve as a powerful reminder that courage is not just about physical bravery but also about standing up for what is right, even in the face of adversity.

Another example of modern courage is seen in the lives of individuals who have overcome significant personal challenges, such as illness, disability, or trauma. These individuals demonstrate incredible resilience and determination, refusing to be defined by their circumstances and instead choosing to live their lives with purpose and hope. Their stories inspire others to find the courage within themselves to face their own challenges and to keep moving forward, no matter how difficult the journey may be.

The Psychology of Courage

The psychology of courage is a fascinating area of study, as it seeks to understand the mental and emotional processes that enable individuals to act bravely in the face of fear or danger. Researchers have found that courage is not a fixed trait but rather a dynamic quality that can be developed and strengthened over time. This understanding of courage as a skill that can be cultivated offers hope to those who may feel that they lack the inner strength to face their fears.

One of the key factors in the development of courage is the ability to manage and regulate fear. Fear is a natural and necessary response to danger, but it can also be paralyzing if not properly managed. Courageous individuals are often able to recognize their fear, acknowledge it, and then take action despite it. This ability to "feel the fear and do it anyway" is a hallmark of courage and is often developed through practice and experience.

Another important aspect of courage is the presence of a strong sense of purpose or conviction. People who are deeply committed to a cause, a belief, or a goal are often more willing to take risks and face challenges because they are driven by something greater than themselves. This sense of purpose provides the motivation and resilience needed to overcome obstacles and persevere in the face of adversity.

Cultivating Courage

Cultivating courage is a lifelong process that involves both self-reflection and action. One of the first steps in developing courage is to identify the areas of our lives where we feel fear or uncertainty and to explore the underlying reasons for these feelings. By understanding the sources of our fear, we can begin to challenge and reframe them, transforming them into opportunities for growth and learning.

Taking small steps toward courage can also be an effective way to build confidence and resilience. This might involve setting incremental goals that push us slightly out of our comfort zones, such as speaking up in a meeting, trying something new, or addressing a difficult situation. Each small act of courage builds on the last, gradually increasing our capacity to face bigger challenges.

Another important aspect of cultivating courage is surrounding ourselves with supportive and encouraging people. Positive relationships can provide us with the strength and encouragement we need to take risks and face our fears. By sharing our struggles and successes with others, we can gain new perspectives and insights, as well as the reassurance that we are not alone in our journey.

The Role of Courage in Relationships

Courage is not just an individual quality; it also plays a vital role in our relationships with others. In relationships, courage is often expressed through vulnerability, honesty, and the willingness to address difficult issues. It takes courage to open up to others, to share our true feelings and experiences, and to be honest about our needs and desires. This type of emotional courage is essential for building deep, meaningful connections with others.

In romantic relationships, for example, courage might involve addressing conflicts or misunderstandings head-on, rather than avoiding them. It takes courage to have difficult conversations, to apologize when we are wrong, and to work through challenges together. This willingness to face issues with honesty and openness can strengthen the bond between partners and create a foundation of trust and respect.

Courage is also important in friendships and family relationships. It takes courage to set boundaries, to stand up for ourselves, and to advocate for our needs. It also takes courage to support others through difficult times, to offer help and guidance when needed, and to be there for them, even when it is not easy. In this way, courage helps to build and maintain the strong, supportive relationships that are essential for our well-being and happiness.

Courage in Creativity and Innovation

Courage is also a driving force behind creativity and innovation. Whether in the arts, sciences, business, or technology, creativity often requires the courage to think differently, to challenge the status quo, and to take risks. Creative individuals and innovators are often willing to step outside of conventional boundaries, to explore new ideas, and to experiment with new approaches, even in the face of uncertainty or potential failure.

In the arts, for example, courage might involve expressing a deeply personal or controversial perspective, creating something entirely new, or breaking away from traditional forms and techniques. This type of creative courage can lead to groundbreaking works that challenge societal norms, provoke thought, and inspire change.

In business and technology, courage is often seen in the willingness to take risks, to innovate, and to pursue bold new ideas. Entrepreneurs and innovators must have the courage to take risks, to embrace uncertainty, and to persevere in the face of obstacles and setbacks. This courage to innovate can lead to significant breakthroughs and advancements that have the potential to change industries and improve lives.

Courage and Ethical Responsibility

Courage is also closely linked to ethical responsibility. In both our personal and professional lives, we are often faced with situations that require us to make difficult ethical decisions. It takes courage to stand up for what is right, to make decisions that align with our values, and to hold ourselves and others accountable for their actions.

In the workplace, for example, ethical courage might involve speaking out against unethical practices, advocating for fair treatment, or making decisions that prioritize the well-being of employees, customers, or the environment, even when it is not the most profitable or convenient option. This type of ethical courage is essential for building trust, integrity, and a positive organizational culture.

In our personal lives, ethical courage might involve making choices that reflect our values and principles, even when they are difficult or unpopular. It might involve standing up for others, speaking out against injustice, or making sacrifices for the greater good. This willingness to act in accordance with our ethical beliefs, even in the face of adversity, is a key aspect of living with integrity and authenticity.

Courage and Legacy

The impact of courage extends beyond our immediate actions and decisions; it also shapes the legacy we leave behind. Courageous individuals often leave a lasting impact on the world, inspiring others to follow in their footsteps and to continue the work they have started. This legacy of courage can be seen in the lives of historical figures, activists, and everyday heroes who have made a difference in their communities and the world.

For example, the legacy of civil rights leader Nelson Mandela continues to inspire generations of activists and advocates for social justice. His courage to stand up against oppression and to fight for equality has left an indelible mark on history, reminding us of the power of courage to create change.

Similarly, the courage of individuals who have overcome personal challenges, such as survivors of illness, trauma, or adversity, can leave a lasting legacy of hope and resilience. Their stories inspire others to find the courage within themselves to face their own challenges and to continue moving forward, no matter how difficult the journey may be.

The Enduring Power of Courage

Courage is what connects our fears to our aspirations, blending our struggles with our triumphs. It is the quiet strength that propels us forward when the path is uncertain, the invisible force that steadies our hands and hearts in the face of adversity. Courage is not the absence of fear, but the mastery of it, the ability to walk boldly into the unknown despite trembling knees and a racing heart.

Courage is a fundamental human quality that has been celebrated throughout history and across cultures. It is the ability to confront fear, pain, danger, uncertainty, or intimidation, and to act with integrity and purpose, even when the odds seem insurmountable. Whether in the grand gestures of historical figures or the quiet persistence of everyday individuals, courage is what enables us to live authentically, to strive for our highest aspirations, and to make a lasting impact on the world.

As we continue to navigate the complexities of life, we can draw strength from the examples of courage that surround us, from the stories of heroes past and present, and from the courage that lies within each of us. By cultivating courage in our own lives, we can face our challenges with resilience and grace, build deep and meaningful relationships, and live with integrity and purpose. In doing so, we not only enrich our own lives but also contribute to a more courageous, just, and compassionate world.

Courage is the lifeblood of heroes and the heartbeat of change. It is the quiet resolve to keep moving forward, to keep trying, and to keep believing in ourselves and our dreams, no matter how difficult the journey may be. Ultimately, courage is what makes us human, what binds us together, and what enables us to reach our greatest potential. Let us embrace courage in all its forms and let it guide us through the challenges and opportunities that lie ahead.

CHAPTER 5
TIME

"Time is a created thing. To say 'I don't have time' is to say 'I don't want to.'" — Lao Tzu

Time: The Silent Architect of Our Existence

Time, the silent architect of our existence, weaves its invisible threads through the fabric of reality, shaping our lives in ways both subtle and profound. It is the great equalizer, the one constant that binds every living being, from the mightiest stars in the cosmos to the smallest creatures on Earth. Time is both our greatest ally and our most formidable adversary, a force that we can neither halt nor control, yet one that defines every moment of our journey.

The Fundamental Nature of Time

Time is one of the most fundamental aspects of our existence, an ever-present force that governs our lives from birth to death. It is the unseen force that shapes the fabric of our lives, guiding our daily rhythm and influencing our experiences. Though intangible and elusive, time is deeply ingrained in our consciousness, influencing our decisions, emotions, and perceptions in ways both subtle and profound. As we move through life, our relationship with time evolves, reflecting our growth, our struggles, and our understanding of the world around us.

From the moment we are born, time begins to assert its presence. We learn to measure it through the cycles of day and night, the changing seasons, and the ticking of clocks. Time becomes a constant companion, dictating the pace of our activities and the structure of our days. As children, time feels abundant and endless, each day a new adventure waiting to be explored. But as we grow older, time seems to accelerate, slipping through our fingers faster and faster, leaving us to grapple with the fleeting nature of our existence.

The Human Endeavor to Measure and Control Time

Throughout history, humans have sought to understand and control time. Ancient civilizations developed calendars to mark the passage of days and seasons, and the invention of the clock revolutionized how we perceive and manage time. The precision of modern timekeeping allows us to synchronize our actions, plan our futures, and reflect on our pasts. Yet, despite our best efforts, time remains an enigma, a force that we can never fully grasp or control. It is both a friend and a foe, a source of comfort and anxiety, a reminder of life's brevity and its infinite possibilities.

The earliest attempts to measure time were deeply rooted in nature. The movement of the sun, the phases of the moon, and the changing seasons provided the first clues to the passage of time. Ancient civilizations like the Egyptians and the Mayans developed complex calendars based on these natural cycles, using them to organize agricultural activities, religious rituals, and social events. These early systems of timekeeping were not just practical tools; they were also imbued with symbolic meaning, reflecting the human desire to find order and meaning in the universe.

The invention of the mechanical clock in the Middle Ages marked a significant turning point in humanity's relationship with time. No longer dependent on the rhythms of nature, people could now measure time with unprecedented precision. The clock became a symbol of modernity and progress, its ticking hands a constant reminder of the relentless march of time. The spread of clocks in public spaces, such as town squares and churches, further emphasized the communal importance of timekeeping as people synchronized their lives to a shared temporal rhythm.

In the modern era, time has become even more precise and regimented, thanks to advances in technology. The development of atomic clocks, which measure time based on the vibrations of atoms, has allowed us to define time with extraordinary accuracy. These clocks are so precise that they would lose less than a second over millions of years. This precision is crucial for a wide range of applications, from global navigation systems to the synchronization of financial markets. Yet, despite our ability to measure time with such accuracy, its true nature remains as elusive as ever.

Cultural Perspectives on Time

In many ways, our relationship with time is shaped by our culture and environment. Different societies have different attitudes toward time, valuing punctuality and efficiency in some cases while prioritizing leisure and reflection in others. The pace of life varies across the globe, with some cultures moving at a frenetic speed and others embracing a more relaxed, unhurried approach. These differences reflect the diverse ways in which people interpret and respond to time, shaping their identities and their experiences of the world.

In Western cultures, time is often viewed as a linear, finite resource that must be managed carefully. The phrase "time is money" encapsulates this attitude, emphasizing the importance of efficiency, productivity, and the avoidance of waste. In this context, time is something to be controlled and optimized, with schedules, deadlines, and timetables dictating the rhythm of daily life. The emphasis on punctuality and time management in Western societies reflects a broader cultural value placed on achievement, progress, and the efficient use of resources.

In contrast, many Eastern cultures view time in a more cyclical and fluid manner. In cultures influenced by Hinduism, Buddhism, and other Eastern philosophies, time is seen as a continuous cycle of birth, death, and rebirth, rather than a linear progression from beginning to end. This perspective is reflected in practices such as meditation and mindfulness, which emphasize being present in the moment rather than constantly striving for future goals. The concept of "karma" in Hindu and Buddhist thought also underscores the cyclical nature of time, as actions in this life are believed to influence future incarnations.

Indigenous cultures around the world also offer unique perspectives on time. Many Indigenous societies emphasize the interconnectedness of time, nature, and community, viewing time not as an individual resource to be managed but as a shared experience that binds people to the land and to each other. In these cultures, time is often marked by natural events, such as the changing of the seasons, the migration of animals, or the flowering of plants. These markers of time are deeply embedded in the community's rituals, stories, and traditions, reflecting a holistic understanding of time as a living, dynamic force.

Time and Personal Development

Time also plays a crucial role in our personal development. As we journey through life, we accumulate memories, experiences, and wisdom, all of which are shaped by the passage of time. Our sense of self is inextricably linked to our perception of time, as we reflect on who we were, who we are, and who we hope to become. Time allows us to learn from our mistakes, to grow from our challenges, and to evolve as individuals. It is through the lens of time that we make sense of our lives, finding meaning and purpose in the moments that matter most.

The passage of time is a key factor in the formation of our identities. From childhood to old age, we go through various stages of development, each marked by its own set of challenges, opportunities, and experiences. These stages are often shaped by cultural expectations and social norms, which provide a framework for understanding our place in the world at different points in our lives. For example, adolescence is typically seen as a time of exploration and self-discovery, while middle age is often associated with career achievements and family responsibilities. Old age, in turn, is often viewed as a time of reflection and wisdom.

As we move through these stages, our relationship with time evolves. In childhood, time seems to stretch out endlessly, with each day offering new possibilities for play and discovery. As we enter adulthood, time becomes more structured and goal-oriented, with the demands of work, family, and personal aspirations often dictating how we spend our days. In old age, time may once again take on a different character, as we reflect on the past and consider the legacy we will leave behind.

Our sense of time is also shaped by our experiences and the way we process them. Positive experiences, such as moments of joy, love, and accomplishment, can make time seem to fly by, while difficult experiences, such as grief, loss, or boredom, can make time feel slow and heavy. This subjective experience of time is influenced by our emotions, our state of mind, and our overall well-being. For example, a person who is deeply engaged in a creative project may lose track of time, experiencing a state of "flow" where time seems to dissolve. In contrast, a person who is dealing with depression or anxiety may feel that time is dragging on interminably.

The Stress and Pressure of Time

Yet, time can also be a source of great stress and pressure. The demands of modern life often leave us feeling overwhelmed by the relentless march of time, as we struggle to balance work, family, and personal aspirations. The fear of wasted time, of missed opportunities, and of unfulfilled potential can weigh heavily on our minds, leading to feelings of regret and dissatisfaction. In a world that moves at an ever-accelerating pace, the challenge of managing time effectively is one that many of us grapple with daily.

The pressure to make the most of our time can lead to a phenomenon known as "time poverty," where individuals feel they have too much to do and not enough time to do it. This sense of time scarcity can create a constant feeling of urgency, as people rush from one task to the next, often sacrificing sleep, relaxation, and leisure in the process. Time poverty is particularly prevalent in modern, urbanized societies, where the demands of work, family, and social obligations can leave little room for personal time.

The emphasis on productivity and efficiency in contemporary society further exacerbates this pressure. In a culture that values achievement and success, time is often equated with money, and the expectation is that every moment should be used productively. This can lead to a sense of guilt or anxiety when we take time for ourselves, whether to rest, relax, or simply enjoy the present moment. The relentless focus on "doing" rather than "being" can make it difficult to appreciate the passage of time and to find meaning in our daily lives.

The impact of time-related stress is not just psychological; it can also have serious physical health consequences. Chronic stress, often fueled by the pressures of time, can lead to a range of health issues, including cardiovascular disease, digestive problems, and weakened immune function. The constant rush to meet deadlines and fulfill obligations can also contribute to burnout, a state of physical and emotional exhaustion that can take a significant toll on both mental and physical well-being.

The Healing Power of Time

Despite these challenges, time also offers us opportunities for growth and renewal. It is through the passage of time that we heal from wounds, both physical and emotional, and find the strength to move forward. Time gives us the space to reflect on our choices, to reassess our goals, and to chart new paths. It is a reminder that life is a journey, not a destination, and that each moment, no matter how fleeting, holds the potential for change and transformation.

The healing power of time is often encapsulated in the saying, "time heals all wounds." While this may not be entirely true—some wounds may never fully heal—time does have a remarkable ability to soften the pain and provide perspective. In the aftermath of a difficult experience, such as the loss of a loved one or a personal failure, time allows us to process our emotions, to grieve, and eventually to begin the process of moving forward. Over time, the intensity of our pain may diminish, and we may find ourselves able to look back with a sense of acceptance, understanding, or even gratitude for the lessons learned.

Time also plays a crucial role in physical healing. The body's natural healing processes are governed by time as cells regenerate, wounds close, and tissues repair themselves. Medical interventions can aid and accelerate this process, but ultimately, healing takes time. This understanding of time as a necessary component of healing is reflected in medical practices and advice, such as the need to rest and recover after surgery, to take time off work during illness, or to allow time for rehabilitation after an injury.

In addition to its role in healing, time also provides us with opportunities for personal growth and transformation. The passage of time allows us to gain new experiences, to learn from our mistakes, and to evolve as individuals. It is through the accumulation of time that we build our knowledge, develop our skills, and deepen our understanding of the world around us. This process of growth and learning is continuous, as each moment offers us the chance to reflect, to make new choices, and to chart new paths.

The Role of Time in Relationships

One of the most profound ways in which we experience time is through our relationships with others. Time spent with loved ones, whether in joy or sorrow, becomes the foundation of our most cherished memories. The bonds we form with family and friends are strengthened by the time we invest in them and the shared experiences that time allows us to create. These connections are a testament to the enduring power of time, as they shape our identities and give our lives meaning.

The importance of time in relationships is evident in the way we prioritize spending time with those we care about. In a world where time is often seen as a scarce resource, the decision to spend time with loved ones is a powerful statement of value and commitment. Whether it is through daily interactions, shared meals, or special occasions, the time we dedicate to our relationships is a key factor in their strength and longevity.

Time also plays a crucial role in the development and deepening of relationships. As we spend more time with others, we come to know them more intimately, understanding their thoughts, feelings, and experiences. This deepening of knowledge and connection can lead to greater empathy, trust, and emotional intimacy. Over time, shared experiences—whether of joy, sorrow, challenge, or triumph—create a bond that is strengthened by the memories and emotions they evoke.

However, time can also be a source of tension in relationships, particularly when it is perceived as insufficient. In the context of busy lives and competing demands, finding the time to nurture relationships can be challenging. The pressures of work, family obligations, and personal goals can make it difficult to prioritize time for relationships, leading to feelings of neglect, frustration, or resentment. Balancing the demands of time in relationships requires careful attention, communication, and a willingness to make compromises.

Time in Philosophy and Spirituality

Moreover, time is a central theme in many philosophical and spiritual traditions. The concept of time as a cyclical, rather than linear, phenomenon is a common thread in many Eastern philosophies, where the cycles of birth, death, and rebirth are seen as part of a continuous, eternal process. In contrast, Western thought often views time as a linear progression with a clear beginning and end. These differing perspectives on time reflect the diversity of human thought and the ways in which we seek to understand our place in the universe.

In ancient Greek philosophy, time was a topic of significant debate. Heraclitus famously declared that "you cannot step into the same river twice," emphasizing the ever-changing nature of time and existence. For Heraclitus, time was a dynamic force, constantly in flux, with no moment ever exactly the same as the one before. This idea of time as a river, flowing continuously and carrying everything along with it, has resonated through the centuries as a powerful metaphor for the human experience of time.

In contrast, the philosopher Parmenides argued that time was an illusion and that reality was unchanging and eternal. For Parmenides, the world of appearances, where time seemed to flow and things seemed to change, was deceptive. The true nature of reality, he claimed, was timeless and unchanging. This perspective challenges the conventional understanding of time, suggesting that what we perceive as the passage of time may be nothing more than an illusion of our senses.

In Eastern philosophies, such as Hinduism and Buddhism, time is often viewed as cyclical. The concept of samsara, or the cycle of birth, death, and rebirth, reflects the belief that time is not linear but repetitive. This cyclical understanding of time is closely linked to the idea of karma, where actions in one life influence the circumstances of future lives. The goal of spiritual practice in these traditions is often to transcend the cycle of samsara and achieve moksha (liberation) or nirvana (enlightenment), states that are beyond time and change.

In Christianity, time is often understood in a linear fashion, with a clear beginning (Creation) and a definitive end (the Second Coming and Final Judgment). This linear perspective on time is also evident in the idea of salvation history, where the events of the Bible are seen as part of a divine plan unfolding through time. The Christian understanding of time is deeply intertwined with the concepts of eternity and eternal life, offering a vision of time that stretches beyond the temporal and into the infinite.

Time in Science: A Fundamental Concept

In the realm of science, time is a fundamental concept that underpins our understanding of the physical world. The theories of relativity and quantum mechanics have revolutionized our understanding of time, challenging our perceptions of its linearity and constancy. Time dilation, the idea that time can slow down or speed up depending on the relative speed and gravity of an observer, has profound implications for our understanding of the universe and our place within it. These scientific discoveries remind us that time is not just a human construct, but a fundamental aspect of the cosmos that shapes the very fabric of reality.

Albert Einstein's theory of relativity fundamentally altered our understanding of time and space. According to Einstein, time is not this absolute, unchanging entity but is relative and can vary depending on the observer's speed and gravitational field. This concept of time dilation means that time can pass more slowly for an object moving at a high velocity or in a strong gravitational field compared to an object at rest or in a weaker gravitational field. This has been experimentally confirmed in various ways, such as through the observation of atomic clocks on fast-moving aircraft or satellites, which tick more slowly than those on the ground.

The implications of time dilation are profound, particularly when considering the nature of the universe and the possibility of space travel. For example, astronauts traveling at near-light speeds would experience time much more slowly than people on Earth, meaning they could potentially return from a long journey to find that many more years had passed on Earth than they had experienced. This concept, often referred to as the "twin paradox," challenges our intuitive understanding of time and highlights the strange and fascinating nature of the universe.

Quantum mechanics also presents a complex and counterintuitive understanding of time. In the quantum realm, particles do not follow a single, well-defined path through time and space but exist in a state of probability, with their positions and velocities only becoming certain when observed. This has led to the concept of "quantum time," where the distinction between past, present, and future becomes blurred, and the idea of a linear flow of time is challenged. Some interpretations of quantum mechanics even suggest that time may not exist at the most fundamental level of reality, raising profound questions about the nature of existence.

The Dual Nature of Time

As we navigate the complexities of time, we are reminded of its dual nature—both a resource to be managed and a mystery to be embraced. Time can be a source of joy, as we celebrate the milestones of our lives, and a source of sorrow, as we mourn the passing of loved ones. It can be a motivator, driving us to achieve our goals, and a comfort, providing the perspective needed to appreciate the present moment. In all its forms, time is a constant companion, guiding us through the ever-changing landscape of our lives.

Time's dual nature is evident in the way it shapes our experiences and emotions. The passage of time can bring healing and growth, but it can also bring loss and decay. We celebrate birthdays, anniversaries, and achievements, marking the passage of time with joy and gratitude. At the same time, we may feel the weight of time's passage in the aging of our bodies, the fading of memories, and the loss of those we love. This duality makes time a source of both hope and melancholy, as we navigate the complex emotions it evokes.

Time also has the power to transform our understanding of experiences and events. What may seem like a tragedy or setback in the moment can, with the passage of time, be seen in a different light. Time allows us to gain perspective, to see the bigger picture, and to understand the deeper meaning of our experiences. It can turn pain into wisdom, failure into growth, and loss into acceptance. This transformative power of time is one of its most profound gifts, offering us the possibility of redemption, renewal, and transformation.

Living with Intention: Making the Most of Time

Ultimately, our relationship with time is a deeply personal one, shaped by our experiences, beliefs, and aspirations. It is a reminder of the impermanence of life, the fleeting nature of each moment, and the importance of living with intention and purpose. As we move forward, it is up to us to decide how we will spend our time—whether we will let it slip through our fingers or seize it with both hands, making the most of each precious second. In the end, time is not just something we measure, but something we live, and it is in the living that we find its true meaning.

Living with intention means making conscious choices about how we use our time. It involves prioritizing what truly matters to us, whether that is relationships, personal growth, creative expression, or contributing to the greater good. It means being mindful of the present moment, appreciating the beauty and richness of life as it unfolds. It also means recognizing the value of time, not just as a resource to be managed, but as a gift to be cherished and savored.

To live with intention is to embrace the present moment, to find joy and meaning in the here and now, rather than constantly striving for the future or dwelling on the past. It is to recognize that each moment is unique and irreplaceable, and to approach life with a sense of gratitude and wonder. By living with intention, we can transform our relationship with time, finding fulfillment and purpose in the rhythm of our days.

In conclusion, time is a multifaceted and profound force that shapes every aspect of our existence. It is the silent architect of our lives, guiding us through the journey of growth, learning, and transformation. Time is both a resource to be managed and a mystery to be embraced, offering us the opportunity to live with intention and purpose. As we navigate the complexities of time, we are reminded of its dual nature—both a source of joy and sorrow, a motivator and a comfort, a force that shapes our experiences and emotions. Ultimately, our relationship with time is a deeply personal one, shaped by our experiences, beliefs, and aspirations. By embracing the present moment, living with intention, and making the most of each precious second, we can find fulfillment and purpose in the rhythm of our days, and discover the true meaning of time.

CHAPTER 6
INTEGRITY

"The best way to find out if you can trust somebody is to trust them." — Ernest Hemingway

Integrity: The key to Ethical Behavior and Personal Character

Integrity is a key to ethical behavior and personal character, embodying the quality of being honest, principled, and unwaveringly committed to moral and ethical standards. It represents a harmony between one's values and actions, and it is the bedrock upon which trust, respect, and credibility are built. Integrity is not just a personal attribute but a vital component of a just and functioning society, influencing how individuals and institutions operate and interact.

The Core of Integrity: Consistency and Honesty

At its core, integrity is about consistency and honesty. It involves aligning one's actions with one's values, even when it is inconvenient or difficult. Integrity requires that individuals remain true to their principles and commitments, irrespective of external pressures or potential rewards. This steadfast adherence to moral principles is crucial for maintaining trust and credibility in both personal and professional relationships. When individuals act with integrity, they demonstrate reliability and authenticity, which fosters trust and strengthens relationships.

Honesty is a fundamental aspect of integrity. It involves being truthful in all situations, whether dealing with minor daily interactions or significant life events. Honest communication and transparency are essential for maintaining integrity. When people are honest, they provide accurate information, acknowledge their mistakes, and avoid deceit. This openness is vital for building and sustaining trust, as it ensures that interactions are grounded in truth and clarity. In professional settings, honesty also means upholding ethical standards and refraining from manipulative or deceptive practices, which can have far-reaching consequences for both individuals and organizations.

The Importance of Accountability in Integrity

Integrity also involves taking responsibility for one's actions. It requires individuals to own up to their mistakes, learn from them, and make amends where necessary. This sense of accountability reflects a commitment to ethical conduct and a willingness to address and rectify errors. It is an important aspect of personal growth and development, as it encourages individuals to reflect on their actions and strive for continuous improvement. By accepting responsibility, individuals demonstrate maturity and a genuine commitment to ethical behavior.

Taking responsibility for one's actions is not just about admitting to mistakes; it also involves making conscious choices that align with one's values. This means thinking critically about the potential impact of one's decisions on others and the broader community. For example, in a professional setting, a leader who takes accountability for a failed project demonstrates integrity by acknowledging the mistakes made, analyzing what went wrong, and implementing corrective measures to prevent future errors. This approach not only fosters a culture of accountability but also strengthens the trust and respect of the team members.

Handling Conflicts of Interest with Integrity

Integrity is reflected in how individuals handle conflicts of interest. It involves making decisions based on fairness and principle rather than personal gain or external pressures. When faced with situations where personal interests conflict with professional or ethical standards, individuals with integrity will prioritize the greater good and adhere to their principles. This commitment to fairness and impartiality is essential for maintaining credibility and ensuring that decisions are made in an ethical and just manner.

Conflicts of interest can arise in various contexts, such as business, politics, or personal relationships. For example, a public official who must make a decision that could benefit a close relative faces a conflict of interest. Acting with integrity would mean recusing oneself from the decision-making process to avoid any appearance of bias or favoritism. In the business world, integrity is demonstrated when a manager chooses to act in the best interest of the company and its stakeholders, even if it means forgoing a personal benefit.

Organizational Integrity: Building a Culture of Trust

In addition to personal integrity, organizational integrity is equally important. Organizations that operate with integrity create a culture of trust and respect, both internally and externally. This involves establishing and enforcing ethical guidelines, promoting transparency, and holding individuals accountable for their actions. Organizations with a strong sense of integrity are more likely to foster positive relationships with stakeholders, including employees, customers, and the community. They are also better equipped to navigate ethical challenges and maintain a positive reputation.

Organizational integrity is not just about complying with laws and regulations; it is about embedding ethical values into the fabric of the organization. This means creating a work environment where ethical behavior is encouraged and rewarded, and where unethical actions are addressed promptly and fairly. For example, an organization that promotes transparency in its financial reporting and ensures that its marketing practices are honest and not misleading demonstrates a commitment to integrity. This not only builds trust with customers and investors but also creates a sense of pride and loyalty among employees.

Leadership and Integrity: Setting the Standard

Integrity plays a crucial role in leadership. Leaders who exhibit integrity serve as role models for others, setting a standard for ethical behavior and decision-making. They inspire confidence and respect by demonstrating consistency between their values and actions. Leaders with integrity are more likely to earn the trust and loyalty of their team, as they are seen as reliable and principled. This trust is essential for effective leadership, as it fosters a positive and productive work environment.

Leadership integrity involves more than just making ethical decisions; it also includes being transparent, admitting mistakes, and being willing to listen to others' perspectives. A leader who embodies integrity is someone who does not shy away from difficult conversations and who prioritizes the well-being of the team and the organization over personal gain. This type of leadership creates a culture where team members feel valued, heard, and supported, which in turn leads to higher levels of engagement and productivity.

Integrity and Personal Fulfillment

Integrity is vital for personal fulfillment and self-respect. Living with integrity means being true to oneself and one's values, which contributes to a sense of inner peace and satisfaction. When individuals act in accordance with their principles, they are more likely to experience a sense of purpose and fulfillment. This alignment between values and actions helps to build self-respect and confidence, as individuals feel that they are living authentically and honorably.

Living with integrity also means making choices that reflect one's true self rather than succumbing to external pressures or societal expectations. For example, an individual who chooses a career path that aligns with their passion and values, rather than one that is merely lucrative or prestigious, is likely to feel more fulfilled and content. This sense of fulfillment is not just about achieving external success; it is about knowing that one is living a life that is true to one's principles and beliefs.

Integrity in a Complex World

In today's world, the importance of integrity cannot be overstated. With the prevalence of misinformation, ethical dilemmas, and complex challenges, maintaining integrity is more crucial than ever. In an era where trust is often in short supply, individuals and organizations that uphold integrity stand out as examples of reliability and credibility. They provide a counterbalance to dishonesty and unethical behavior, contributing to a more just and trustworthy society.

The digital age has brought about new challenges to integrity, particularly in the realms of information sharing and communication. The rapid spread of misinformation and the pressure to present a curated, idealized version of oneself online can lead to ethical compromises. Maintaining integrity in this environment requires a commitment to honesty and transparency, as well as a critical awareness of the impact of one's actions on others. This might involve being mindful of the information one shares, ensuring that it is accurate and truthful, and resisting the temptation to engage in deceitful or manipulative online behaviors.

The Courage to Uphold Integrity

However, maintaining integrity is not always easy. It requires courage and resilience, especially when faced with temptations or pressures to compromise one's values. It also involves making difficult decisions and standing firm in one's principles, even in the face of adversity. Despite these challenges, the rewards of living with integrity are profound. It leads to stronger relationships, greater respect, and a more fulfilling life.

The courage to uphold integrity often involves standing up for what is right, even when it is unpopular or when there are significant risks involved. For example, a whistleblower who exposes unethical practices within an organization demonstrates integrity by prioritizing ethical principles over personal safety or job security. This type of courage is not just about making grand gestures; it can also be seen in everyday actions, such as refusing to participate in gossip, standing up to bullying, or speaking out against injustice.

The Rewards of Living with Integrity

The rewards of living with integrity are manifold. On a personal level, individuals who consistently act with integrity experience a sense of self-respect and inner peace that comes from knowing they are living in alignment with their values. This self-respect is a powerful motivator, as it reinforces the importance of maintaining integrity in all areas of life. Additionally, living with integrity fosters a sense of trust and respect from others, which can lead to stronger, more meaningful relationships.

In a professional context, individuals who demonstrate integrity are often seen as trustworthy and reliable, which can open up opportunities for career advancement and leadership roles. Organizations that operate with integrity are more likely to attract and retain top talent, as employees are drawn to workplaces that prioritize ethical behavior and create a culture of respect and accountability.

Moreover, the impact of integrity extends beyond the individual or organization. When integrity is upheld in society, it contributes to the creation of a more just and equitable world. Ethical behavior and decision-making at all levels—from individual actions to corporate policies and government regulations—help to build a society where trust, fairness, and justice are the norm.

Real-Life Stories of Integrity

Integrity, the quality of being honest and having strong moral principles, is often demonstrated through real-life stories where individuals or groups choose to do the right thing, even when it is difficult or when no one is watching. These stories serve as powerful examples of the impact that integrity can have on individuals, communities, and society as a whole.

One well-known story of integrity involves the actions of Rosa Parks, whose refusal to give up her seat on a segregated bus in Montgomery, Alabama, in 1955 became a pivotal moment in the civil rights movement. Parks' act of defiance was not just a spontaneous decision; it was a deliberate choice to stand up for justice and equality, even in the face of personal risk. Her courage and integrity inspired others to take action and helped to galvanize the movement for civil rights in the United States.

Another example of integrity can be found in the actions of whistleblowers who risk their careers and personal safety to expose unethical practices within organizations. One such individual is Dr. Jeffrey Wigand, a former tobacco executive who exposed the industry's knowledge of the harmful effects of smoking and its efforts to manipulate nicotine levels to increase addiction. Wigand's decision to speak out, despite the threats and legal battles he faced, was a powerful demonstration of integrity and a commitment to the public good.

In the business world, integrity is exemplified by companies that prioritize ethical practices over short-term profits. For example, Patagonia, an outdoor clothing company, has built its brand on a commitment to environmental sustainability and social responsibility. The company has taken bold steps, such as donating 100% of its Black Friday sales to environmental causes and encouraging customers to repair and reuse their products rather than buying new ones. Patagonia's integrity in its business practices has earned it a loyal customer base and a reputation as a leader in corporate social responsibility.

Challenges to Integrity in Modern Society

While the importance of integrity is widely recognized, there are significant challenges to upholding this value in modern society.

The pressures of competition, the pursuit of success, and the complexities of ethical dilemmas can all lead individuals and organizations to compromise their integrity. Additionally, the rise of digital media and the rapid spread of information have created new challenges for maintaining integrity, as misinformation and unethical behavior can easily proliferate.

One of the key challenges to integrity is the pressure to succeed at any cost. In highly competitive environments, whether in business, sports, or academia, the temptation to cut corners, bend the rules, or engage in unethical behavior can be strong. This pressure is often compounded by societal expectations and the fear of failure. However, the long-term consequences of compromising integrity—such as loss of trust, damage to reputation, and legal repercussions—far outweigh any short-term gains.

Another challenge to integrity is the complexity of ethical dilemmas. In a globalized world where decisions can have far-reaching impacts, it is not always easy to determine the right course of action. Ethical dilemmas often involve competing values and interests, making it difficult to uphold integrity while balancing other considerations. For example, a business leader may face a dilemma between maximizing profits and ensuring fair labor practices in a supply chain. Navigating these dilemmas requires careful consideration, transparency, and a commitment to ethical principles.

The Role of Education in Fostering Integrity

Education plays a crucial role in fostering integrity, both in individuals and in society as a whole. By teaching ethical principles, critical thinking skills, and the importance of honesty and accountability, educators can help students develop a strong sense of integrity that will guide their actions throughout their lives.

Ethics education should begin early, with lessons on honesty, fairness, and responsibility integrated into the curriculum from a young age. As students progress through their education, they should be encouraged to think critically about ethical issues and to consider the impact of their actions on others. This can be done through discussions, case studies, and real-life examples that challenge students to grapple with complex ethical questions.

In higher education and professional training programs, integrity should be emphasized as a core value. This includes not only teaching the importance of ethical behavior but also providing students with the tools and frameworks they need to navigate ethical dilemmas in their chosen fields. For example, medical schools often include training on medical ethics, while business schools may offer courses on corporate social responsibility and ethical leadership.

The Impact of Integrity on Society

The impact of integrity extends far beyond individual actions; it has profound implications for society as a whole. When integrity is upheld at all levels—by individuals, organizations, and governments—it creates a foundation of trust, fairness, and justice that is essential for a healthy and functioning society.

In a society where integrity is valued and practiced, people are more likely to trust one another, institutions are more likely to operate transparently and fairly, and justice is more likely to be upheld. This creates a positive feedback loop, where trust and integrity reinforce each other, leading to greater social cohesion and stability.

Conversely, when integrity is lacking, the consequences can be severe. Corruption, dishonesty, and unethical behavior erode trust, undermine institutions, and create a sense of cynicism and disillusionment. This can lead to a breakdown in social order, increased conflict, and a loss of faith in the ability of society to function justly.

The Enduring Value of Integrity

Integrity is a fundamental aspect of ethical behavior and personal character. It involves honesty, accountability, fairness, and consistency between one's values and actions. Integrity is essential for building trust, maintaining credibility, and fostering positive relationships. It is also crucial for personal fulfillment and effective leadership. In a world where ethical challenges are prevalent, upholding integrity is vital for creating a just and trustworthy society. By embracing and practicing integrity, individuals, and organizations contribute to a more ethical and harmonious world.

Living with integrity is not always easy, but it is always worthwhile. It requires courage, resilience, and a commitment to ethical principles, even in the face of challenges. However, the rewards of living with integrity—stronger relationships, greater respect, and a more fulfilling life—are profound.

In the end, integrity is not just about doing the right thing when others are watching; it is about doing the right thing, even when no one is watching. It is about living in a way that is true to oneself and to one's values, and it is about creating a world where trust, fairness, and justice are the norm. By upholding integrity in all areas of life, we can contribute to a better, more ethical, and more just society.

CHAPTER 7
CHANGE

"If you don't like something, change it. If you can't change it, change your attitude." — Maya Angelou

The Inevitability and Power of Transformation

Change is an inevitable and constant force in life, shaping our experiences, relationships, and the world around us. It is the process through which growth, evolution, and progress occur, challenging us to adapt, innovate, and reconsider our perspectives. While change can often be met with resistance or fear, it is also a powerful catalyst for transformation, offering opportunities for renewal and the discovery of new possibilities.

At its core, change is about movement—a shift from one state of being to another. This movement can be gradual or sudden, predictable or unexpected. In some cases, change is a deliberate choice, driven by a desire for improvement or a response to an opportunity. In others, it is imposed upon us by external circumstances, forcing us to navigate uncharted waters and adapt to new realities. Regardless of its origin, change demands flexibility and resilience, qualities that are essential for navigating the complexities of life.

The Nature of Change

Change is a multifaceted concept, encompassing a wide range of experiences and phenomena. It can manifest in various forms, from the subtle shifts in our daily routines to the monumental transformations that alter the course of our lives. Understanding the nature of change requires recognizing its different dimensions, including its pace, scope, and impact.

Change can occur gradually, unfolding over time in a way that allows us to adjust incrementally. This type of change is often less jarring and can be easier to manage. For example, the aging process is a gradual change that we all experience. As we age, our bodies, minds, and perspectives shift slowly, allowing us to adapt to new realities at a manageable pace. Similarly, learning a new skill or habit often involves gradual change as we practice and refine our abilities over time.

Sudden change, on the other hand, can be more challenging to cope with. These changes happen quickly, often without warning, and can disrupt our sense of stability and security. Events such as the loss of a loved one, a sudden job loss, or an unexpected health diagnosis can thrust us into situations that demand immediate adaptation. While these changes can be difficult, they also offer opportunities for growth and resilience, as we are forced to confront new realities and find ways to navigate them.

Predictable vs. Unpredictable Change

Some changes are predictable, allowing us to anticipate and prepare for them. For example, the changing of the seasons is a predictable cycle that we experience every year. We know that winter will eventually give way to spring, and we can prepare for this transition by adjusting our clothing, activities, and routines accordingly. Similarly, life stages such as graduating from school, starting a career, or retiring are predictable changes that many people experience. These transitions, while significant, are often expected and can be planned for in advance.

Unpredictable change, however, can catch us off guard and challenge our ability to adapt. Natural disasters, economic downturns, and global pandemics are examples of unpredictable changes that can have far-reaching effects on our lives. These events often require us to respond quickly and creatively, finding new ways to cope with unforeseen circumstances. While unpredictable change can be unsettling, it also offers opportunities for innovation and resilience as we learn to navigate uncharted territory.

Personal Growth Through Change

One of the most profound aspects of change is its ability to bring about personal growth. When we embrace change, we open ourselves up to learning and development. We step outside our comfort zones, challenging the status quo and exploring new horizons. This process of adaptation often leads to greater self-awareness, as we are forced to confront our fears, limitations, and preconceptions. Through change, we discover strengths we never knew we had and develop skills that enhance our ability to thrive in an ever-evolving world.

Embracing the Unknown

Personal growth through change often involves embracing the unknown. This can be a daunting prospect, as it requires us to step into unfamiliar territory and face the uncertainty of what lies ahead. However, it is precisely this willingness to explore the unknown that fosters growth and development. By pushing our boundaries and challenging ourselves, we create opportunities for new experiences and insights.

For example, consider the experience of moving to a new city or country. This type of change can be both exciting and intimidating, as it involves leaving behind the familiar and venturing into the unknown. However, the process of adapting to a new environment, meeting new people, and navigating a different culture can lead to significant personal growth. We may develop greater resilience, adaptability, and cultural awareness, as well as a deeper understanding of ourselves and our place in the world.

Overcoming Fear and Resistance

Fear is a natural response to change, particularly when it involves stepping outside our comfort zones or facing uncertain outcomes. However, overcoming this fear is essential for personal growth. When we allow fear to hold us back, we limit our potential and miss out on opportunities for learning and development. By confronting our fears and embracing change, we build confidence and resilience, which in turn enable us to navigate future challenges more effectively.

One way to overcome fear and resistance to change is to reframe our perspective. Instead of viewing change as a threat, we can choose to see it as an opportunity for growth and discovery. This shift in mindset can help us approach change with curiosity and openness rather than fear and anxiety. Additionally, seeking support from others, whether through friends, family, or professional guidance—can provide us with the encouragement and resources we need to navigate change successfully.

Change as a Catalyst for Transformation

In many cases, change serves as a catalyst for profound personal transformation. When we are faced with significant life events or transitions, we are often forced to reevaluate our values, priorities, and goals. This process of introspection can lead to a deeper understanding of ourselves and a clearer sense of purpose.

For example, consider the experience of going through a major life change, such as a career transition or the end of a significant relationship. These types of changes can be incredibly challenging, as they often involve letting go of the familiar and embarking on a new path. However, they also offer the opportunity for personal transformation. By reflecting on our experiences and considering what we truly want out of life, we can make conscious choices that align with our values and aspirations.

In this way, change can serve as a powerful catalyst for self-discovery and personal growth. It encourages us to let go of old patterns and habits that no longer serve us and to embrace new possibilities for the future. By navigating change with intention and openness, we can create a life that is more authentic, fulfilling, and aligned with our true selves.

The Impact of Change on Relationships

Change also plays a critical role in shaping relationships. As individuals grow and evolve, so too do their connections with others. Relationships that once seemed unbreakable may falter in the face of change, while new bonds may form as people find common ground in shared experiences. Change tests the resilience of relationships, revealing their true nature and challenging individuals to communicate, compromise, and support one another through the process of transformation.

Evolving Relationships

Relationships are dynamic and constantly evolving. As individuals change and grow, their relationships must also adapt to these changes. This can be both a challenging and rewarding process. On one hand, change can strain relationships, as individuals 'needs, desires, and perspectives shift over time. For example, a couple that has been together for many years may find that their interests, goals, and values have diverged, leading to tension and conflict. Similarly, friendships may be tested when one person undergoes significant life changes, such as moving to a new city or starting a new career.

On the other hand, change can also bring people closer together. Shared experiences of change, whether positive or negative, can create bonds between individuals. These shared experiences provide opportunities for empathy, compassion, and connection. For example, a family that goes through a challenging time together, such as coping with a loss or navigating a difficult transition, may emerge from the experience with a stronger sense of unity and support.

Navigating Change in Relationships

Navigating change in relationships requires effective communication, empathy, and flexibility. When individuals are open and honest about their experiences and feelings, they can work together to find common ground and support one another through the process of change. This may involve making compromises, setting new boundaries, or finding new ways to connect and strengthen the relationship.

It is also important to recognize that not all relationships are meant to last forever. As individuals grow and change, they may outgrow certain relationships or find that their connections with others no longer serve their needs. While this can be a painful realization, it is also an opportunity for growth and transformation. By letting go of relationships that no longer align with our values or goals, we make space for new connections that are more supportive and fulfilling.

Change as an Opportunity for New Connections

Change often brings new people and experiences into our lives, offering opportunities for new connections and relationships. For example, starting a new job or moving to a new city can introduce us to new colleagues, friends, and communities. These new connections can enrich our lives and provide us with fresh perspectives, ideas, and opportunities for growth.

Additionally, shared experiences of change can create strong bonds between individuals. Whether it is going through a challenging experience together, such as surviving a natural disaster or navigating a major life transition, or simply sharing the excitement of a new adventure, these experiences can deepen our connections with others and create lasting relationships

The Role of Change in Societal Progress

In a broader context, change is a driving force behind societal progress. History is marked by moments of significant change, where old systems, beliefs, and structures are challenged and replaced by new ideas and ways of living. Social, political, and technological changes have all played pivotal roles in shaping the world we live in today. While these changes often come with growing pains, they are essential for addressing the needs and aspirations of an evolving society.

Social Movements and Change

Social movements have been instrumental in driving societal change throughout history. These movements often arise in response to injustices, inequalities, or unmet needs within society. They challenge existing power structures, advocate for new ideas and values, and mobilize individuals and communities to take action.

Consider the environmental movement, which has gained momentum since the 1960s. This global effort has focused on addressing issues like pollution, deforestation, and climate change. Pioneering individuals like Rachel Carson, whose landmark book "Silent Spring" sparked widespread public concern about pesticides and pollution, played a crucial role. The movement has led to significant legislative reforms, such as the establishment of Earth Day, the creation of the Environmental Protection Agency in the U.S., and the signing of international agreements like the Paris Climate Accord. These efforts continue to push for sustainable practices and policies to protect our planet for future generations.

Similarly, the women's rights movement has been a driving force for change, advocating for gender equality and challenging traditional gender roles and stereotypes. Through activism, advocacy, and legal reforms, the movement has made significant progress in securing women's rights to education, employment, and political representation. While there is still much work to be done, the movement has had a profound impact on society, shifting cultural norms and opening up new opportunities for women.

Technological Change and Its Impact on Society

Technological advancements have also played a crucial role in driving societal change. Innovations in technology have transformed the way we live, work, and communicate, creating new industries, altering economies, and connecting people across the globe.

For example, the advent of the internet and digital technology has revolutionized the way we access and share information, communicate with others, and conduct business. These changes have created new opportunities for economic growth and innovation, but they have also raised important ethical and social questions, such as issues of privacy, security, and the digital divide.

Similarly, advances in medical technology have had a profound impact on society, improving health outcomes and extending life expectancy. Innovations such as vaccines, antibiotics, and advanced medical treatments have saved countless lives and improved the quality of life for millions of people. However, these advancements have also raised complex ethical questions about access to healthcare, the cost of medical treatment, and the implications of emerging technologies such as genetic engineering and artificial intelligence.

Political Change and Societal Progress

Political change is another important aspect of societal progress. Throughout history, political revolutions, reforms, and movements have brought about significant changes in governance and leadership. These changes have often been driven by the desire for greater freedom, equality, and justice.

For example, the American Revolution was a pivotal moment in history, challenging the colonial rule of the British Empire and establishing a new nation based on the principles of liberty, democracy, and self-governance. Similarly, the French Revolution sought to overthrow the monarchy and establish a more egalitarian society, advocating for the rights of the individual and the principles of liberty, equality, and fraternity.

In more recent history, the fall of the Berlin Wall and the subsequent collapse of the Soviet Union marked a significant political change, signaling the end of the Cold War and the spread of democratic governance in Eastern Europe. These events had a profound impact on the global political landscape, reshaping international relations and influencing the course of history.

The Emotional Landscape of Change

Navigating change is an emotional journey. It can evoke a wide range of feelings, from excitement and anticipation to anxiety and grief. The emotional landscape of change is complex, as individuals must process the loss of the familiar while embracing the uncertainty of the new.

Fear is a common emotional response to change, particularly when it involves stepping into the unknown or facing uncertain outcomes. The fear of failure, loss, or rejection can hold us back from fully embracing change and exploring new possibilities. However, fear is not inherently negative—it is a natural response that can serve as a signal that we are stepping into new territory and pushing our limits.

Anxiety often accompanies fear, as we grapple with the uncertainty and unpredictability of change. This anxiety can manifest in physical symptoms, such as tension, restlessness, and difficulty concentrating, as well as emotional symptoms, such as worry, irritability, and a sense of unease. Managing anxiety during times of change requires self-awareness, coping strategies, and support from others.

Grief and Loss

Grief is another emotion that often accompanies change, particularly when it involves letting go of something or someone we once held dear. This could be a place, a relationship, a role, or a stage of life. Grieving these losses is a natural part of the process, allowing us to honor what was while making space for what is to come.

For example, the transition from one stage of life to another—such as from adolescence to adulthood, or from working life to retirement—can evoke feelings of grief as we let go of familiar roles and identities. Similarly, the end of a significant relationship, whether through a breakup, divorce, or the death of a loved one, can lead to profound feelings of loss and sadness.

Navigating grief during times of change requires patience, self-compassion, and the support of others. It is important to allow ourselves to feel and process these emotions rather than suppressing or denying them. By acknowledging and honoring our grief, we can begin to heal and move forward.

Excitement and Hope

While change can evoke challenging emotions, it can also bring feelings of excitement and hope. The promise of new opportunities, experiences, and growth can be exhilarating as we anticipate the possibilities that lie ahead. Embracing these positive emotions can help us stay motivated and resilient as we navigate the challenges of change.

For example, starting a new job, moving to a new city, or embarking on a new adventure can fill us with excitement and a sense of possibility. These experiences offer opportunities for personal growth, new connections, and the chance to explore new interests and passions. By focusing on the positive aspects of change, we can cultivate a sense of optimism and hope that helps us navigate the uncertainties of the journey.

Strategies for Embracing Change

Given the inevitability of change, it is important to develop strategies for embracing it. By cultivating a growth mindset, building resilience, and taking a proactive approach to change, we can not only survive but thrive in an ever-changing world.

Cultivating a Growth Mindset

A growth mindset is the belief that our abilities, intelligence, and potential can be developed through effort, learning, and persistence. This mindset is essential for embracing change, as it encourages us to view challenges and setbacks as opportunities for growth and development rather than as threats to our self-worth.

To cultivate a growth mindset, we can start by reframing our perspective on change. Instead of viewing change as something to be feared or avoided, we can choose to see it as an opportunity for discovery, learning, and personal transformation. By approaching change with curiosity and openness, we create space for new experiences and insights that can enrich our lives.

Additionally, embracing a growth mindset involves embracing the process of learning and growth rather than focusing solely on outcomes or results. This means being willing to take risks, make mistakes, and learn from our experiences, even when the path is uncertain or challenging. By focusing on the journey rather than the destination, we can develop greater resilience, adaptability, and confidence in our ability to navigate change.

Building Resilience

Resilience is the ability to adapt to change and bounce back from adversity. It is a crucial skill for navigating the ups and downs of life, allowing us to maintain our well-being and thrive in the face of challenges.

Building resilience involves developing a range of coping skills and strategies that help us manage stress, regulate our emotions, and maintain a positive outlook. These strategies may include practices such as mindfulness, exercise, and healthy communication, as well as seeking support from others when needed.

One important aspect of resilience is the ability to reframe our perspective on change and adversity. Instead of viewing challenges as insurmountable obstacles, we can choose to see them as opportunities for growth and learning. This shift in mindset allows us to approach challenges with a sense of empowerment and agency rather than feeling overwhelmed or defeated.

Taking a Proactive Approach to Change

Finally, embracing change requires us to be proactive. Rather than waiting for change to happen to us, we can take an active role in shaping our own lives and creating the changes we want to see.

This might involve setting goals, making plans, and taking steps to create the changes we desire, whether in our personal lives, careers, or communities. By being proactive, we can take control of our own destiny and create a life that aligns with our values and aspirations.

Additionally, being proactive in the face of change involves staying informed and adaptable. This means staying open to new information, perspectives, and opportunities and being willing to adjust our plans and strategies as needed. By remaining flexible and open to change, we can navigate the uncertainties of life with greater ease and confidence.

Ultimately, change is a fundamental part of the human experience. It shapes who we are and who we become, both as individuals and as a collective. By embracing change, we can harness its potential to drive personal growth, strengthen relationships, and contribute to the ongoing evolution of society. Change is not something to be feared, but rather, a powerful force that, when embraced, can lead to a richer, more fulfilling life.

The inevitability of change means that it is not something we can avoid, but it is something we can learn to navigate and embrace. By developing the skills, mindset, and resilience needed to handle change, we can not only survive but thrive in an ever-changing world. Whether in our personal lives, relationships, or the broader societal context, change is a powerful force for growth, innovation, and progress. Embracing change allows us to live fully, adapt gracefully, and continuously evolve as we journey through life.

As we move forward in our own lives and as members of a broader society, it is essential to recognize the power of change and our capacity to shape it. By approaching change with intention, resilience, and a commitment to growth, we can create a future that is not only different but better, richer, and more aligned with our deepest values and aspirations.

CHAPTER 8
HOPE

"You may say I'm a dreamer, but I'm not the only one. I hope someday you'll join us. And the world will live as one." — John Lennon

The Nature of Hope

Hope is one of the most powerful and enduring forces within the human spirit. It is the belief that things can and will improve, even when circumstances seem bleak. Hope transcends the present moment, reaching beyond the limitations of the here and now, and envisions a future filled with possibility. It is the spark that ignites our will to persevere, the light that guides us through the darkness, and the anchor that keeps us steady when life's storms threaten to overwhelm us.

At its core, hope is an emotional and psychological state that involves a positive expectation for the future. It is not merely wishful thinking or blind optimism; rather, it is a deep-seated belief that, despite the challenges and uncertainties we face, there is the potential for a better outcome. Hope is often linked to resilience, as it empowers individuals to continue striving towards their goals and dreams, even when faced with obstacles.

Hope is a dynamic and multifaceted emotion that can be influenced by both internal and external factors. Internally, hope is shaped by our beliefs, values, and experiences. It is nurtured by a sense of purpose and direction, which gives us something to hold onto during difficult times. Externally, hope can be reinforced by the support of others, positive feedback, and witnessing the success of others in similar situations.

Hope in Times of Difficulty

Perhaps the most profound expression of hope is found in times of difficulty and hardship. When faced with illness, loss, or personal struggle, hope becomes a crucial survival mechanism. It provides the strength to endure pain and suffering, offering the belief that better days lie ahead. In this context, hope is not just a passive state of mind; it is an active force that drives individuals to seek solutions, find comfort, and continue fighting, even when the odds seem insurmountable.

During times of adversity, hope serves as a way forward, even when the path is unclear. It gives individuals the courage to face their challenges head-on, to endure hardship with grace, and to find meaning in their experiences. This type of hope is often deeply personal and can be rooted in spirituality, faith, or a sense of connection to something greater than oneself.

Hope as a Catalyst for Personal Growth

Hope also plays a significant role in personal development and growth. It is the belief that we have the capacity to change, to learn, and to become better versions of ourselves. This type of hope encourages us to set goals, to aspire to new heights, and to believe in our ability to overcome challenges. It is the foundation upon which dreams are built, and it motivates us to take the necessary steps toward achieving our ambitions.

Personal growth is often a journey marked by setbacks, failures, and moments of self-doubt. Hope acts as a compass during these times, guiding us back to our true north and reminding us of the potential that lies within us. It fuels our perseverance, helping us to stay committed to our goals, even when progress is slow or obstacles seem insurmountable.

Hope in Relationships

Building strong, supportive relationships can also help to nurture hope. When we are connected to others who believe in us and offer encouragement, it reinforces our own belief in the possibility of a better future. Social support is a key component of hope, as it provides both emotional and practical resources to help us navigate challenges.

Relationships play a critical role in sustaining hope, particularly during difficult times. The encouragement and support of loved ones can provide the strength and motivation needed to keep going, even when the journey is tough. By surrounding ourselves with positive, supportive individuals, we create an environment where hope can flourish.

Despite misunderstandings or conflicts, we can find common ground and strengthen our bonds. Hope allows us to see the potential in others, to believe in the power of love, and to work towards building healthy, meaningful connections with those around us. It is the glue that holds relationships together during difficult times and the catalyst for reconciliation and growth.

Hope in relationships also involves a shared vision for the future. It is the belief that, together, we can overcome challenges and build a life that reflects our shared values and aspirations. This collective hope fosters resilience within relationships, helping partners to navigate conflicts and challenges with a sense of optimism and mutual support.

Hope as a Force for Collective Progress

Hope is also a driving force in our vision for the future, both individually and collectively. It is the belief that, despite the challenges facing humanity, there is a path forward that leads to progress, justice, and peace. This form of hope inspires action, encouraging people to work towards positive change in their communities and the world at large. It is the force behind social movements, innovations, and efforts to create a better world for future generations.

Throughout history, hope has been the catalyst for social change and collective progress. It has inspired leaders, activists, and ordinary individuals to challenge the status quo, to fight for justice and equality, and to envision a world where everyone can thrive. This type of hope is rooted in a belief in the inherent goodness of humanity and the potential for collective action to bring about positive change.

Hope and Mental Health

Hope is closely linked to mental and emotional well-being. It provides a buffer against despair, anxiety, and depression, helping individuals cope with difficult situations. When people feel hopeful, they are more likely to take positive actions, seek help when needed, and remain engaged in life, even during tough times.

In the face of stress and trauma, hope serves as a vital coping mechanism. It allows individuals to maintain a sense of purpose and direction, even when their current circumstances are challenging. Hope encourages adaptive coping strategies, such as problem-solving, seeking social support, and finding meaning in adversity. This, in turn, helps to reduce the impact of stress on mental health.

Hope in the Context of Recovery

In the context of recovery from illness, addiction, or psychological distress, hope plays a critical role. It is the belief that recovery is possible that motivates individuals to engage in treatment, to adhere to prescribed interventions, and to continue striving for improvement, even when progress is slow. Hope is often what keeps people going when they feel like giving up, providing the strength to keep moving forward, one step at a time.

Recovery is often a long and challenging process, marked by setbacks and moments of doubt. Hope provides the motivation to persevere through these challenges, to stay committed to the recovery journey, and to believe in the possibility of a better future. It is a lifeline for those in recovery, offering a sense of hope and purpose that sustains them through the ups and downs of the process.

Hope and Resilience

Resilience, the ability to bounce back from adversity, is closely tied to hope. Hope fuels resilience by providing a vision of a better future, which in turn motivates individuals to persist in the face of challenges. People who are hopeful tend to be more resilient because they believe in the possibility of positive outcomes, even in difficult situations. This belief enables them to navigate setbacks and emerge stronger on the other side.

Resilience is not just about enduring hardship; it is about thriving in the face of adversity. Hope plays a central role in this process by providing the motivation to keep going, even when the journey is tough. It helps individuals to maintain a positive outlook, to stay focused on their goals, and to find meaning and purpose in their experiences.

Cultivating Hope

While hope is a natural and often spontaneous emotion, it can also be cultivated and nurtured. One of the most effective ways to cultivate hope is by setting realistic, achievable goals. When we have something to work towards, it gives us a sense of purpose and direction. Achieving small goals can build confidence and reinforce the belief that progress is possible, thereby strengthening hope.

Focusing on positive aspects of life and maintaining an optimistic outlook can help to nurture hope. While it's important to acknowledge challenges and difficulties, choosing to focus on potential solutions and opportunities can shift our perspective and foster a hopeful mindset. Practicing gratitude is another way to cultivate hope. By recognizing and appreciating the good things in our lives, we reinforce the belief that positive outcomes are possible.

Gratitude helps to shift our focus from what is lacking to what is present, creating a foundation for hope to thrive.

Hope as a Lifelong Practice

Hope is a powerful and enduring force that sustains us through life's challenges and uncertainties. It is the belief in the possibility of a better future that motivates us to keep striving, to keep believing, and to keep moving forward. Whether in times of adversity, personal growth, or collective progress, hope provides the light that guides us through the darkness and the strength that helps us persevere.

Cultivating hope is a lifelong practice, one that requires intentional effort and a commitment to nurturing a positive mindset. By setting goals, practicing gratitude, building supportive relationships, and focusing on the positive aspects of life, we can create a foundation for hope to thrive. This practice of hope not only sustains us through difficult times but also empowers us to live a life filled with purpose, joy, and fulfillment.

The Universal Nature of Hope

Hope is a universal human experience, one that transcends cultures, languages, and geographic boundaries. It is a force that connects us to one another, reminding us of our shared humanity and our collective potential for growth and change. Whether we are facing personal challenges or working towards collective progress, hope is the thread that weaves us together, guiding us towards a brighter future.

Throughout history, hope has been a source of strength and inspiration for individuals and communities around the world. It has fueled social movements, inspired acts of bravery and compassion, and sustained people through the darkest of times. This universal nature of hope is a testament to its enduring power and its ability to uplift and unite us, no matter where we come from or what challenges we face.

Hope and the Future

As we look to the future, hope will continue to play a critical role in shaping our individual and collective destinies. It is hope that inspires us to dream big, to set ambitious goals, and to work towards a better world. Whether we are working towards personal growth, social change, or global progress, hope is the force that propels us forward, guiding us towards a future filled with possibility.

Hope is not just about waiting for a better future to arrive; it is about actively working to create that future. By cultivating hope in our own lives and in our communities, we can contribute to a world that is more compassionate, just, and hopeful. This commitment to hope is a powerful act of resistance against despair and a declaration of our belief in the potential for positive change.

The Enduring Legacy of Hope

Hope is not just a fleeting emotion or a temporary state of mind; it is an enduring legacy that we leave behind for future generations. The hope we cultivate in our own lives, the hope we inspire in others, and the hope we contribute to our communities all leave a lasting impact on the world. This legacy of hope is a gift to future generations, a reminder that no matter how dark the night is, there is always a dawn.

As we continue to navigate the challenges of life, let us remember the enduring power of hope. Let us cultivate hope in our own lives, inspire hope in others, and work towards a future filled with possibility. By embracing hope as a guiding principle, we can create a legacy that is filled with love, compassion, and the belief in a better tomorrow.

The Light of Hope

Hope is the belief in the possibility of a better future that motivates us to keep striving, to keep believing, and to keep moving forward. Whether in times of adversity, personal growth, or collective progress, hope provides the light that guides us through the darkness and the strength that helps us persevere. By cultivating hope in our lives, we can build resilience, foster mental and emotional well-being, and create a brighter future for ourselves and those around us.

CHAPTER 9
CREATIVITY

"Creativity is intelligence having fun." — Albert Einstein

The Vital Force of Creativity: Shaping Human Experience and Progress

Creativity is a fundamental aspect of the human experience, a powerful force that drives innovation, expression, and progress. It is the ability to transcend traditional ideas, rules, and patterns to create something new and meaningful. Whether in art, science, business, or daily life, creativity fuels our capacity to solve problems, communicate ideas, and transform the world around us. It is the spark that ignites our imagination and enables us to bring our unique visions to life.

At its essence, creativity is about thinking differently. It is the process of looking at the world from new perspectives, finding connections where none seem to exist, and envisioning possibilities beyond the conventional. This often involves breaking free from established norms and embracing uncertainty. Creativity thrives in environments where curiosity, experimentation, and risk-taking are encouraged, allowing individuals to explore uncharted territories and challenge the status quo.

Creativity is not confined to a single domain or discipline. It is a multifaceted process that can manifest in a variety of forms, from the creation of a beautiful painting or an evocative piece of music to the development of an innovative technological solution or a novel scientific theory. At its core, creativity involves a deep engagement with the world around us, a willingness to ask questions and an openness to exploring new ideas.

The Creative Process: Inspiration and Persistence

The creative process is not linear; it is often marked by moments of inspiration followed by periods of trial and error. Creativity requires patience and perseverance, as it involves navigating through ambiguity and setbacks. It is in these moments of struggle that creativity often flourishes as the mind is pushed beyond previously perceived limits. The willingness to embrace failure as part of the creative journey is crucial, as each misstep provides valuable insights and opportunities for growth.

Inspiration often strikes in unexpected moments, whether through observation, reflection, or sudden insight. However, creativity does not rely solely on these moments of inspiration. It also requires discipline and persistence. Creative individuals often engage in iterative processes, refining and revising their ideas until they reach a point of clarity and coherence. This process of refinement is where creativity and craftsmanship intersect, as ideas are shaped and molded into their final form.

Creativity in the Arts: Expression and Connection

Creativity manifests in countless ways, from the arts to the sciences, from the personal to the professional. In the arts, creativity is the lifeblood of expression. It is what enables artists, writers, musicians, and performers to convey emotions, tell stories, and connect with audiences on a profound level. Through creative expression, we explore the human condition, communicate complex ideas, and foster empathy. The arts serve as a mirror to society, reflecting its values, struggles, and triumphs, and inspiring change.

Artistic creativity is not just about producing aesthetically pleasing works; it is also about engaging with deeper themes and ideas. Whether through a painting that challenges societal norms, a novel that explores the complexities of human relationships, or a piece of music that evokes powerful emotions, creative works have the ability to move us, to make us think, and to inspire action. The arts offer a space for experimentation and innovation, where traditional boundaries can be pushed and new forms of expression can emerge.

Creativity in Science and Technology: Innovation and Discovery

In the sciences and technology, creativity is equally vital. It drives innovation, leading to breakthroughs that shape our understanding of the world and improve our quality of life. Scientific discoveries, technological advancements, and engineering feats all begin with creative thinking—the ability to ask "what if?" and "why not?" Creativity in these fields often involves reimagining existing concepts, developing new methodologies, and pushing the boundaries of what is possible.

Scientific creativity often involves thinking beyond the current paradigms and envisioning new ways of understanding complex phenomena. It requires a combination of analytical thinking and imaginative insight, allowing scientists and researchers to explore new hypotheses, design innovative experiments, and develop groundbreaking theories. Technological creativity, on the other hand, involves the application of these scientific insights to create new tools, devices, and systems that solve practical problems and enhance human capabilities.

Creativity in Everyday Life: Problem-Solving and Adaptability

Creativity is not limited to the realms of art and science; it plays a significant role in everyday life and decision-making. From finding new ways to solve problems at work to discovering creative approaches to parenting, creativity helps us navigate the complexities of life. It encourages flexibility, adaptability, and resourcefulness, enabling us to overcome challenges and seize opportunities.

In everyday life, creativity can manifest in simple yet profound ways. It might involve finding a creative solution to a scheduling conflict, developing a new recipe from available ingredients, or inventing a game to entertain children. These acts of creativity are not necessarily about producing something tangible but about thinking differently and approaching situations with an open mind. By embracing creativity in our daily lives, we can enhance our problem-solving abilities, improve our relationships, and find joy in the ordinary.

Creativity in Business: Innovation and Competitive Advantage

Moreover, creativity is essential in the business world, where it drives innovation and competitive advantage. Companies that foster a culture of creativity are more likely to develop groundbreaking products, services, and strategies. Creative leadership is crucial in this context, as it involves inspiring teams to think outside the box, encouraging diverse perspectives, and cultivating an environment where experimentation is valued.

In the business world, creativity is not just about generating new ideas; it is also about implementing those ideas effectively. Creative leaders must balance the need for innovation with the practical considerations of business operations, such as resource allocation, market dynamics, and customer needs. By fostering a culture of creativity, businesses can stay ahead of the curve, adapt to changing market conditions, and create value for their customers and stakeholders.

Collaborative Creativity: The Power of Collective Effort

However, creativity is not just an individual trait; it is also a collective phenomenon. Collaborative creativity can lead to extraordinary outcomes as different minds bring together their unique experiences and insights. When people work together creatively, they can achieve more than they could individually, generating ideas and solutions that are more innovative and comprehensive.

Collaborative creativity involves harnessing the diverse perspectives and talents of a group to achieve a common goal. This process often requires effective communication, mutual respect, and a willingness to consider alternative viewpoints. By working together creatively, teams can leverage their collective strengths to tackle complex challenges, develop innovative solutions, and drive progress.

The Challenges of Creativity: Vulnerability and Risk-Taking

While creativity is often celebrated, it can also be challenging. The creative process can be daunting, as it requires vulnerability and the willingness to take risks. Creative individuals often face uncertainty, criticism, and self-doubt. However, it is precisely this willingness to embrace the unknown that makes creativity so powerful. It is through creative exploration that we discover new possibilities, break down barriers, and contribute to the ever-evolving tapestry of human knowledge and culture.

Creativity often involves stepping outside of one's comfort zone and challenging established norms. This can be a vulnerable experience, as it exposes individuals to the possibility of failure and criticism. However, it is also through this process of taking risks and experimenting with new ideas that creativity flourishes. By embracing vulnerability and being open to failure, creative individuals can push the boundaries of what is possible and achieve remarkable outcomes.

Creativity in a Rapidly Changing World

In a rapidly changing world, creativity is more important than ever. It equips us with the tools to adapt to new realities, solve complex problems, and envision a better future. Creativity is not a luxury; it is a necessity. It empowers us to dream, to innovate, and to make our mark on the world. Whether through a masterpiece of art, a groundbreaking scientific discovery, or a simple solution to a daily challenge, creativity is the force that propels us forward, enabling us to shape our destinies and enrich our lives.

As the world continues to evolve, the need for creative thinking will only increase. Global challenges such as climate change, economic inequality, and technological disruption require innovative solutions that transcend traditional approaches. By cultivating creativity, we can develop the skills and mindsets needed to navigate these challenges and create a more sustainable, equitable, and prosperous future.

The Future of Creativity

Looking ahead, the role of creativity in shaping the future cannot be overstated. As technology continues to advance and societal challenges become more complex, the ability to think creatively will be a critical skill for individuals and organizations alike. Creativity will drive innovation in fields such as artificial intelligence, biotechnology, and renewable energy, leading to new breakthroughs that will transform our world.

At the same time, the creative arts will continue to play a vital role in reflecting and shaping the human experience. Artists, writers, musicians, and performers will explore new forms of expression, pushing the boundaries of what is possible and inspiring audiences with their creative visions. In this way, creativity will remain a driving force in our cultural and intellectual evolution.

Embracing Creativity

Creativity is the spark that ignites our imagination and enables us to bring our unique visions to life. Whether in art, science, business, or daily life, creativity fuels our capacity to solve problems, communicate ideas, and transform the world around us.

As we navigate the complexities of life and the challenges of a rapidly changing world, creativity will remain an essential tool for shaping our destinies and enriching our lives. By embracing creativity, we can unlock new possibilities, break down barriers, and contribute to the ever-evolving tapestry of human knowledge and culture. Creativity is not just a luxury or a pastime; it is a necessity, a driving force that propels us forward and enables us to make our mark on the world.

CHAPTER 10
SUCCESS

"Success is not the key to happiness. Happiness is the key to success. If you love what you are doing, you will be successful." — Albert Schweitzer

The Multifaceted Nature of Success: A Personal and Evolving Journey

Success is a multifaceted concept that holds different meanings for different people shaped by individual values, goals, and experiences. For some, success may be measured in terms of wealth, power, or status, while for others, it may be defined by personal fulfillment, happiness, or the positive impact they have on others. Despite these varied definitions, success generally represents the achievement of a desired goal or the realization of one's aspirations. It is the culmination of effort, perseverance, and sometimes a bit of luck, and it often requires overcoming obstacles and challenges along the way.

Defining Success: A Personal Vision

At its core, success is about setting and achieving goals. Whether those goals are related to career advancement, personal growth, relationships, or any other area of life, success begins with a clear vision of what one wants to accomplish. This vision provides direction and motivation, serving as a roadmap for the journey ahead. However, success is not just about the destination; it is also about the process of striving toward that goal. The journey itself is often where the most significant learning and growth occur.

Each person's definition of success is unique, reflecting their individual values and priorities. For some, success may mean reaching a high level of professional achievement, such as becoming a leader in their field or running a successful business. For others, success might be more intimately tied to personal relationships, such as raising a family, cultivating deep friendships, or contributing to their community. Still, others may define success in terms of personal development, such as achieving inner peace, mastering a skill, or overcoming personal challenges.

Perseverance: The Foundation of Success

One of the key ingredients of success is perseverance. The path to success is rarely straightforward or easy. It is often filled with setbacks, failures, and moments of doubt. Those who achieve success are typically those who are able to push through these challenges, maintaining their focus and determination even when the going gets tough. Perseverance involves a commitment to one's goals and a refusal to give up, even when progress seems slow or obstacles appear insurmountable. It is the ability to stay the course, adapt to changing circumstances, and continue moving forward, one step at a time.

Perseverance is not just about enduring hardship but also about maintaining a proactive attitude toward achieving one's goals. It requires the mental fortitude to keep striving, even when faced with repeated failures. Successful people understand that setbacks are not the end of the road but rather opportunities to learn and grow. By maintaining resilience and a long-term perspective, they are able to persist through challenges and eventually achieve their goals.

Risk-Taking: Stepping Out of the Comfort Zone

Another important aspect of success is the willingness to take risks. Success often requires stepping out of one's comfort zone and embracing uncertainty. This might involve making difficult decisions, trying something new, or taking a leap of faith. Risk-taking is inherently uncomfortable because it involves the possibility of failure. However, without taking risks, it is difficult to achieve anything truly significant. Successful people understand that failure is not the opposite of success but rather a part of the process. Each failure provides valuable lessons that can be used to refine strategies and improve future outcomes.

Taking risks is often a key factor in achieving breakthroughs, whether in business, art, science, or personal development. It involves challenging the status quo, exploring uncharted territories, and daring to dream big. By embracing risk, individuals open themselves up to new opportunities and possibilities that they might not have encountered otherwise. Successful people are those who are willing to bet on themselves, take calculated risks, and learn from the outcomes, whether positive or negative.

Resilience: Bouncing Back from Adversity

Success is also closely tied to resilience. Resilience is the ability to bounce back from adversity and to keep going in the face of challenges. It involves maintaining a positive attitude, staying motivated, and not allowing setbacks to derail progress. Resilient individuals are able to view challenges as opportunities for growth and learning, rather than as insurmountable barriers. This mindset allows them to stay focused on their goals and to continue making progress, even in difficult circumstances.

Resilience is not just about enduring hardship but about thriving in the face of adversity. It is about using challenges as stepping stones to greater success. Resilient individuals are those who can maintain their focus and optimism even when the going gets tough. They are able to adapt to changing circumstances, learn from their experiences, and keep moving forward with determination and purpose.

The Role of a Strong Work Ethic in Success

In addition to perseverance, risk-taking, and resilience, success often requires a strong work ethic. Hard work is a fundamental component of success, as it is through sustained effort and dedication that goals are achieved. This means consistently putting in the time and energy required to make progress, even when it is difficult or inconvenient. It also involves a commitment to excellence, striving to do one's best in every endeavor, and not settling for mediocrity.

A strong work ethic is characterized by discipline, focus, and a willingness to go the extra mile. It involves setting high standards for oneself and being willing to put in the effort required to meet those standards. Successful people understand that there are no shortcuts to success; it requires consistent, sustained effort over time. By cultivating a strong work ethic, they are able to build the skills, knowledge, and experience needed to achieve their goals.

The Importance of Support

However, success is not just about individual effort. It is also about relationships and the support of others. Success is rarely achieved in isolation; it often involves collaboration, teamwork, and the encouragement of mentors, peers, and loved ones. Building strong, supportive relationships can provide the guidance, resources, and motivation needed to achieve success. It is important to recognize and appreciate the contributions of others, as well as to give back and support those who are on their own journeys toward success.

Supportive relationships provide the emotional and practical support needed to navigate the challenges of the journey toward success. Whether it is the encouragement of a mentor, the feedback of a colleague, or the love of family and friends, these relationships play a crucial role in helping individuals stay motivated and focused. Successful people understand the importance of building and maintaining strong relationships and are willing to invest the time and effort required to nurture these connections.

Success Beyond External Measures: The Role of Fulfillment

While external measures of success, such as wealth, status, or recognition, are often emphasized in society, it is important to remember that true success is deeply personal. It is about living in alignment with one's values, pursuing meaningful goals, and finding fulfillment in the process. For some, this may mean achieving financial security or professional recognition; for others, it may mean cultivating strong relationships, making a positive impact on the world, or simply living a life of purpose and contentment.

Success is not just about achieving external markers of success but also about finding a sense of inner fulfillment and satisfaction. It is about living in a way that is true to oneself, and that reflects one's values and priorities. This might involve pursuing a career that is aligned with one's passions, building meaningful relationships, or contributing to the well-being of others. True success is not just about what one achieves but also about how one feels about their achievements.

The Dynamic Nature of Success

Success is a deeply personal and dynamic concept, one that evolves over time as individuals grow, learn, and change. It is not a static achievement but a continuous journey that requires ongoing effort, reflection, and adaptation. Success can be seen as a measure of how well one lives up to one's potential, how effectively one pursues one's goals, and how meaningfully one contributes to the world around them.

As individuals grow and change, so too does their definition of success. What might have been considered a success at one stage of life may no longer hold the same significance later on. This evolution is a natural part of the journey as people reassess their priorities, set new goals, and continue to strive for growth and improvement. Successful individuals are those who are willing to reflect on their progress, make adjustments as needed, and stay committed to their journey.

Self-Awareness: The Key to Personal Success

An essential aspect of success is self-awareness. Understanding one's strengths, weaknesses, passions, and values is crucial in defining what success means on an individual level. Self-awareness allows people to set goals that are aligned with their true desires and to pursue paths that are fulfilling and authentic. It also enables them to recognize when they are off course and to make the necessary adjustments to realign with their vision of success.

Self-awareness is the foundation of personal success, as it allows individuals to make choices that are aligned with their true selves. By understanding their own motivations, strengths, and areas for growth, individuals can set goals that are meaningful and achievable. Self-awareness also enables individuals to recognize when they are straying from their path and to take corrective action to get back on track.

The Power of a Growth Mindset

Success is also influenced by the mindset with which one approaches life. A growth mindset—the belief that abilities and intelligence can be developed through hard work, learning, and perseverance—is a powerful driver of success. This mindset encourages individuals to embrace challenges, persist in the face of setbacks, and view effort as a path to mastery. In contrast, a fixed mindset—the belief that abilities are static and unchangeable—can hinder success by fostering a fear of failure and a reluctance to take risks.

A growth mindset is characterized by a willingness to learn, a focus on improvement, and an openness to feedback. It involves seeing challenges as opportunities for growth and viewing effort as an essential part of the journey. By cultivating a growth mindset, individuals are more likely to persist through setbacks, take risks, and ultimately achieve their goals. This mindset is a key factor in achieving long-term success, as it fosters resilience, adaptability, and a commitment to continuous improvement.

Prioritization and Time Management in the Pursuit of Success

Another crucial factor in success is the ability to set and maintain priorities. With countless demands on time and energy, focusing on what truly matters is key to achieving meaningful success. This often involves making difficult choices, such as saying no to certain opportunities or activities to focus on those that align with one's goals. Prioritization also means recognizing that success in one area of life, such as a career, should not come at the expense of other important areas, such as health, relationships, or personal well-being.

Time management is closely related to the idea of prioritization. Successfully managing time involves not only planning and organization but also the discipline to follow through on those plans. Effective time management allows individuals to make the most of their opportunities, ensuring that they are consistently working toward their goals. It also helps to reduce stress and create a sense of balance, which is essential for long-term success.

Purpose: The Driving Force Behind Success

Success is often accompanied by a strong sense of purpose. A clear sense of purpose provides direction and motivation, making it easier to stay focused and committed even when faced with challenges. Purpose is what gives meaning to success, transforming it from a mere collection of achievements into a fulfilling and impactful journey. Those who have a strong sense of purpose are more likely to experience lasting success, as they are driven by something greater than themselves.

Purpose is the compass that helps individuals navigate the journey toward success. It provides the motivation to keep going, even when the road is difficult. By aligning their goals with their sense of purpose, individuals can find deeper meaning in their work and in their lives. This sense of purpose not only drives success but also ensures that success is fulfilling and meaningful.

Adaptability: Navigating Change and Uncertainty

Another important element of success is adaptability. The ability to adapt to changing circumstances, learn from experiences, and remain open to new ideas is crucial in a world that is constantly evolving. Adaptability allows individuals to navigate uncertainty and to seize opportunities as they arise. It also fosters innovation, as those who are adaptable are more likely to experiment with new approaches and to find creative solutions to problems.

Adaptability is essential for success in a rapidly changing world. It involves being open to new experiences, willing to learn from failure, and flexible in the face of change. By cultivating adaptability, individuals can navigate the challenges of life with greater ease and find new opportunities for growth and success. Adaptable individuals are those who are able to thrive in uncertain environments, continually learning and evolving as they move toward their goals.

Resilience: The Key to Long-Term Success

Resilience, too, plays a significant role in success. Life is full of setbacks, and the ability to recover from these setbacks, learn from them, and keep moving forward is essential for achieving long-term success. Resilience is not just about bouncing back from failure; it's about using challenges as opportunities for growth and development. Resilient individuals are able to maintain their optimism and determination, even in the face of adversity, which allows them to continue pursuing their goals.

Resilience is the key to long-term success. It involves maintaining a positive attitude, staying focused on one's goals, and persevering through challenges. Resilient individuals are those who are able to navigate setbacks with grace, using them as opportunities to learn and grow. By cultivating resilience, individuals can achieve lasting success, even in the face of adversity.

Success as a Personal Journey

Ultimately, success is not a one-size-fits-all concept. It is defined by each individual based on their unique aspirations and circumstances. What matters most is that one feels a sense of accomplishment and satisfaction in their achievements, whatever they may be. Success is a journey, not a destination, and it is found in the pursuit of one's passions, the overcoming of obstacles, and the continual striving to be the best version of oneself. By setting meaningful goals, working hard, taking risks, and maintaining resilience, anyone can achieve success on their own terms and lead a fulfilling, purposeful life.

Success is a deeply personal journey, one that is shaped by an individual's values, goals, and experiences. It is about finding fulfillment in the pursuit of one's passions, achieving personal growth, and making a positive impact on the world. By defining success on one's own terms, individuals can create a life that is meaningful, fulfilling, and aligned with their true selves.

The Importance of Balance in Success

Finally, success is deeply intertwined with a sense of balance. True success is not just about achieving external markers of success, such as wealth or recognition, but also about cultivating inner well-being. This involves maintaining a balance between work and personal life, between ambition and contentment, and between striving for goals and appreciating the present moment. Balance helps to ensure that the pursuit of success does not lead to burnout or neglect of other important aspects of life.

Balance is essential for sustainable success. It involves making time for self-care, nurturing relationships, and finding joy in the present moment. By cultivating balance, individuals can achieve success that is not only meaningful but also sustainable over the long term. Balance ensures that the pursuit of success does not come at the expense of one's health, relationships, or overall well-being.

The Dynamic and Personal Nature of Success

In conclusion, success is a complex concept that encompasses much more than mere achievement. It is about setting meaningful goals, maintaining a positive mindset, managing time effectively, and being adaptable and resilient in the face of challenges. Success is also about living with purpose, maintaining a sense of balance, and continually striving to grow and improve. Ultimately, success is a deeply personal journey, one that requires self-awareness, perseverance, and a commitment to living in alignment with one's true values and aspirations. By embracing the dynamic and personal nature of success, individuals can create a life that is fulfilling, meaningful, and aligned with their deepest values and goals.

CHAPTER 11
HAPPINESS

"Happiness is not having what you want. It is appreciating what you have." — Anonymous

The Pursuit of Happiness: A Journey Towards Fulfillment and Well-Being

Happiness is one of the most sought-after and cherished experiences in human life. It is an emotion, a state of being, and a fundamental aspect of well-being that transcends cultures, ages, and backgrounds. Despite its universal appeal, happiness can be elusive, with its definition and pathways varying greatly from person to person. At its core, happiness is often described as a deep sense of contentment, fulfillment, and joy, arising from positive experiences, meaningful relationships, and a life aligned with one's values and desires.

The Dynamic Nature of Happiness

Happiness is not a constant state but rather a dynamic and fluctuating experience. It can be momentary, sparked by a specific event or achievement, or more sustained, arising from a general sense of well-being and life satisfaction. This duality reflects the distinction between hedonic and eudaimonic happiness. Hedonic happiness refers to the pleasure and enjoyment derived from sensory experiences, material gains, and immediate gratifications. It is the type of happiness one feels when indulging in a delicious meal, receiving a compliment, or experiencing a thrilling adventure.

On the other hand, eudaimonic happiness is rooted in living a meaningful and purposeful life. It is the deeper sense of fulfillment that comes from pursuing long-term goals, personal growth, and contributing to something larger than oneself. This form of happiness is not merely about feeling good at the moment but about living in alignment with one's true self, values, and aspirations. It often involves self-reflection, overcoming challenges, and striving for excellence, leading to a more profound and enduring sense of happiness.

The Role of Relationships in Happiness

One of the key components of happiness is the quality of our relationships. Human beings are inherently social creatures, and strong, supportive connections with others are crucial for our emotional well-being. Positive relationships provide love, support, and a sense of belonging, all of which contribute significantly to happiness. Whether it's the bond between family members, the companionship of friends, or the intimacy of a romantic relationship, these connections are vital sources of joy and comfort.

Moreover, relationships provide a context within which individuals can express themselves, share experiences, and receive validation and support. The emotional richness and security derived from these relationships can buffer against life's stresses and challenges, making us more resilient and better able to cope with difficulties. This social support network is a fundamental pillar of lasting happiness, providing a foundation upon which individuals can build a fulfilling and balanced life.

The Power of Kindness and Compassion

Additionally, acts of kindness and compassion towards others can greatly enhance our own happiness. Helping others, whether through small gestures or significant efforts, can create a sense of purpose and fulfillment. This is because giving to others activates areas of the brain associated with pleasure, trust, and social connection. Furthermore, knowing that one has positively impacted someone else's life fosters a sense of self-worth and contributes to a more meaningful existence.

Kindness and compassion are not only beneficial for those who receive them but also for those who practice them. Engaging in altruistic behaviors has been shown to increase feelings of happiness and satisfaction. This reciprocal relationship between giving and receiving creates a cycle of positivity that can significantly enhance overall well-being. By making kindness a regular practice, individuals can cultivate a deeper sense of connection with others and a more profound sense of personal fulfillment.

Autonomy and Control

Another essential factor in happiness is a sense of autonomy and control over one's life. Feeling empowered to make decisions, pursue goals, and shape one's destiny is fundamental to experiencing happiness. When individuals feel that they have control over their lives and that their actions align with their values, they are more likely to experience a sense of satisfaction and contentment. This is why personal freedom, the ability to express oneself, and the opportunity to pursue passions are so closely linked to happiness.

Autonomy allows individuals to live authentically, making choices that reflect their true selves and leading lives that are congruent with their personal values. This sense of agency is critical in fostering a sense of purpose and meaning, which are essential components of long-term happiness. By taking ownership of their lives and making decisions that align with their deepest values, individuals can create a life that is fulfilling, meaningful, and truly their own.

Mindset and Attitude

Happiness is also closely tied to one's mindset and attitude toward life. A positive outlook, characterized by gratitude, optimism, and resilience, can significantly influence one's happiness. Gratitude, in particular, is a powerful tool for enhancing happiness. By focusing on the positive aspects of life and appreciating what one has rather than dwelling on what is lacking, individuals can cultivate a greater sense of contentment. Optimism, or the tendency to expect positive outcomes, can also contribute to happiness by fostering hope and motivation, even in the face of challenges.

Gratitude shifts the focus from what is missing to what is present, fostering a mindset of abundance rather than scarcity. By regularly practicing gratitude, individuals can enhance their overall sense of well-being and create a positive cycle of thought that supports happiness. Similarly, optimism encourages a forward-looking perspective, allowing individuals to remain hopeful and motivated, even when faced with setbacks. These attitudes not only enhance day-to-day happiness but also build resilience against life's inevitable challenges.

Resilience: The Backbone of Happiness

Resilience, the ability to bounce back from adversity, plays a crucial role in maintaining happiness. Life is full of ups and downs, and the way we respond to setbacks can determine our overall happiness. Resilient individuals are able to navigate difficulties with grace, viewing challenges as opportunities for growth rather than insurmountable obstacles. This mindset not only helps to preserve happiness during tough times but also contributes to long-term well-being by fostering a sense of inner strength and self-efficacy.

Resilience is not just about enduring hardship; it's about thriving in spite of it. It involves developing a mindset that embraces challenges as learning opportunities and views failures as stepping stones to success. By cultivating resilience, individuals can maintain their happiness even in the face of life's inevitable difficulties. This adaptability and strength are key to sustaining long-term well-being and achieving a balanced and fulfilling life.

Personal Growth and Self-Actualization

Another important aspect of happiness is the pursuit of personal growth and self-actualization. Engaging in activities that challenge us, stimulate our minds, and allow us to develop new skills can lead to a deeper sense of fulfillment. Whether through education, hobbies, or creative endeavors, the pursuit of mastery and self-improvement provides a sense of purpose and achievement, both of which are integral to happiness.

Personal growth involves continually striving to better oneself, whether through learning new skills, exploring new interests, or setting and achieving personal goals. This pursuit of growth not only enhances self-esteem and confidence but also contributes to a deeper sense of fulfillment and satisfaction. By continually seeking out new challenges and opportunities for self-improvement, individuals can create a life that is rich, dynamic, and deeply rewarding.

The Role of Physical Well-Being in Happiness

It is also worth noting that happiness is influenced by physical well-being. Regular exercise, a balanced diet, sufficient sleep, and good health contribute to overall happiness. Physical activity, in particular, is known to release endorphins, the body's natural mood lifters, which can enhance feelings of happiness and reduce stress. Taking care of one's body is, therefore, an important component of a happy and fulfilling life.

Physical well-being is the foundation upon which emotional and psychological well-being are built. By maintaining a healthy lifestyle, individuals can enhance their overall sense of well-being and create a strong foundation for lasting happiness. Regular exercise, a nutritious diet, and adequate sleep are all essential components of this foundation, providing the energy, vitality, and mental clarity needed to navigate life's challenges and enjoy its pleasures.

Embracing the Full Spectrum of Emotions

It is important to recognize that happiness is not about constantly feeling joyful or avoiding negative emotions. Life is inherently complex, and experiencing a range of emotions, including sadness, anger, and frustration, is a natural part of the human experience. These emotions can provide valuable insights into our needs, desires, and the changes we need to make in our lives. True happiness does not come from suppressing negative emotions but from embracing them as part of the journey and finding ways to navigate them constructively.

Embracing the full spectrum of emotions allows individuals to live authentically and fully, experiencing life in all its richness and complexity. By acknowledging and accepting negative emotions, individuals can gain deeper insights into their own needs and desires, allowing them to make meaningful changes and grow as individuals. This emotional intelligence is key to achieving long-term happiness, as it enables individuals to navigate life's challenges with grace and resilience.

The Influence of Culture and Society on Happiness

Happiness is also shaped by cultural and societal factors. Different cultures have different conceptions of happiness and different pathways to achieving it. In some cultures, happiness may be closely tied to social harmony and community, while in others, it may be more closely linked to individual achievement and personal fulfillment. Understanding these cultural influences can provide valuable insights into the diverse ways in which happiness is experienced and pursued around the world.

Societal expectations and norms also play a role in shaping our understanding of happiness. In some societies, happiness is equated with material success and external achievements, while in others, it is more closely associated with inner peace and contentment. These cultural and societal influences can shape our perceptions of happiness and the pathways we choose to pursue it. By becoming aware of these influences, individuals can make more informed choices about how to cultivate happiness in their own lives.

The Importance of Mindfulness and Presence

Mindfulness, the practice of being fully present in the moment, is another powerful tool for enhancing happiness. By cultivating mindfulness, individuals can develop a greater awareness of their thoughts, feelings, and experiences, allowing them to engage with life more fully and deeply. Mindfulness encourages a non-judgmental awareness of the present moment, helping individuals to let go of negative thoughts and emotions and to cultivate a sense of peace and acceptance.

Mindfulness also helps individuals to savor positive experiences and to appreciate the simple pleasures of life. By being fully present, individuals can deepen their connection to the world around them, enhancing their overall sense of well-being and happiness. This practice of mindfulness can be cultivated through meditation, yoga, or simply by taking a few moments each day to pause, breathe, and connect with the present moment.

Happiness as a Lifelong Journey

In the end, happiness is a rich and multi-dimensional concept that encompasses much more than fleeting moments of pleasure. It is a state of being that arises from living a life of meaning, connection, and purpose. By nurturing positive relationships, practicing gratitude, pursuing personal growth, and maintaining a healthy and balanced lifestyle, individuals can cultivate a deeper and more lasting sense of happiness. Ultimately, happiness is a personal and evolving journey, one that is shaped by our choices, attitudes, and the way we engage with the world around us.

Happiness is not a destination but a journey, one that requires ongoing effort, reflection, and growth. It is a dynamic and evolving experience shaped by the choices we make and the way we respond to life's challenges. By embracing the journey of happiness and cultivating the attitudes and practices that support it, individuals can create a life that is fulfilling, meaningful, and deeply satisfying.

Cultivating a Life of Happiness

In conclusion, happiness is a wide range of emotions, experiences, and attitudes. It is not just about feeling good in the moment but about living a life that is aligned with one's values, aspirations, and desires. By cultivating positive relationships, practicing kindness and compassion, and maintaining a sense of autonomy and control, individuals can create a strong foundation for lasting happiness.

Happiness is also influenced by one's mindset and attitude, with gratitude, optimism, and resilience playing key roles in sustaining well-being. Physical well-being, personal growth, and mindfulness are also important components of a happy and fulfilling life. By embracing the full spectrum of emotions and understanding the cultural and societal influences on happiness, individuals can make more informed choices about how to pursue happiness in their own lives.

Ultimately, happiness is a lifelong journey, one that requires ongoing effort, reflection, and growth. It is a dynamic and evolving experience shaped by the choices we make and the way we respond to life's challenges. By embracing this journey and cultivating the attitudes and practices that support happiness, individuals can create a life that is fulfilling, meaningful, and deeply satisfying.

CHAPTER 12
WISDOM

"A wise man can learn more from a foolish question than a fool can learn from a wise answer." — Bruce Lee

The Essence of Wisdom: A Pathway to Fulfillment and Harmony

Wisdom is often associated with deep understanding, sound judgment, and the ability to navigate complex situations with grace and clarity. It goes beyond mere knowledge or intelligence; wisdom involves the integration of experience, reflection, and insight to make decisions that are not only effective but also aligned with ethical and moral principles. It is a virtue that has been celebrated across cultures and throughout history, recognized as essential for leading a meaningful and fulfilled life.

Understanding the Deeper Truths: The Core of Wisdom

At its core, wisdom is the ability to see beyond the surface of things and to understand the deeper truths and principles that govern human existence. It is the capacity to discern what is truly important in life, to prioritize long-term well-being over short-term gains, and to act in ways that promote harmony, justice, and compassion. Wisdom involves not just knowing what to do but understanding why it should be done and how it can be done in a way that respects the dignity and rights of others.

This deeper understanding comes from a synthesis of knowledge, experience, and ethical considerations. Wise individuals are able to see the interconnectedness of events and decisions, recognizing that actions have consequences that ripple through the fabric of society. They understand that true success is not measured by material wealth or external validation but by the impact one has on others and the world. This broader perspective allows them to make decisions that are not only practical but also meaningful, contributing to a life that is rich in purpose and significance.

The Role of Experience in Cultivating Wisdom

One of the key aspects of wisdom is its connection to experience. Wisdom is often described as the fruit of lived experience, the knowledge and understanding that come from facing life's challenges, learning from mistakes, and observing the consequences of one's actions over time. Unlike mere information or academic knowledge, which can be acquired through study, wisdom is deeply personal and experiential. It is shaped by the trials and tribulations of life, by the successes and failures that teach us what truly matters and how to navigate the complexities of the world.

Experience provides the raw material from which wisdom is crafted. Through experience, individuals learn about the nuances of human behavior, the complexities of moral dilemmas, and the unpredictability of life. They gain insights into the patterns and rhythms of life, recognizing the ebb and flow of challenges and opportunities. Over time, these experiences accumulate, forming a rich tapestry of understanding that allows individuals to approach life's challenges with a sense of calm and assurance.

Reflection: The Gateway to Deeper Understanding

Reflection is another critical component of wisdom. Experience alone does not automatically lead to wisdom; it must be accompanied by thoughtful reflection on those experiences. Wisdom involves the ability to step back from the immediacy of situations, to consider different perspectives, and to contemplate the broader implications of one's actions. This reflective process allows individuals to distill the lessons of their experiences into deeper understanding, helping them to make better decisions in the future.

Reflective practice involves taking the time to analyze one's experiences, to explore the motivations and outcomes of actions, and to consider how different choices might have led to different results. It is through this process of reflection that individuals can gain insights into the nature of their own behavior, the dynamics of relationships, and the ethical dimensions of decision-making. Reflection allows individuals to learn from their past, to grow from their experiences, and to apply these lessons to future situations.

The Role of Humility in Wisdom

Wisdom is also closely tied to humility. Wise individuals recognize the limits of their knowledge and understanding. They are aware that they do not have all the answers and that there is always more to learn. This humility allows them to approach life with an open mind, to listen to others, and to be receptive to new ideas and perspectives. Humility in wisdom also means being willing to admit when one is wrong and to change course when necessary. It is the understanding that true wisdom is not about always being right but about being willing to grow and evolve.

Humility in wisdom fosters a mindset of continuous learning and growth. It allows individuals to remain open to feedback, to seek out new information, and to adapt to changing circumstances. This openness to learning is a hallmark of wise individuals who understand that wisdom is not a static trait but a dynamic process of growth and development. Humility also allows individuals to approach life with a sense of curiosity and wonder, recognizing that there is always more to discover and learn.

The Ethical Dimensions of Wisdom

Compassion and empathy are also integral to wisdom. A wise person understands the interconnectedness of all people and recognizes that their actions have an impact on others. This awareness leads to a compassionate approach to decision-making, one that considers the needs, feelings, and well-being of others.

Wisdom is not just about making good decisions for oneself; it is about contributing to the greater good and acting in ways that promote the welfare of others. Empathy, the ability to put oneself in another's shoes, is essential for understanding the human experience and for making choices that are fair, just, and kind.

Compassionate wisdom involves recognizing the humanity in others and making decisions that honor and respect that humanity. It requires individuals to consider the impact of their actions on others and to strive to make choices that promote the well-being of all. This ethical dimension of wisdom is what allows wise individuals to act with integrity and to contribute positively to the world around them. By cultivating compassion and empathy, individuals can develop a deeper understanding of the human experience and make decisions that are aligned with their values and the greater good.

Perspective: Seeing the Bigger Picture

In addition to these qualities, wisdom involves a sense of perspective. Wise individuals are able to see the bigger picture to understand how the present moment fits into the broader context of life. They are not easily swayed by immediate emotions or pressures but are able to take a long-term view, considering the future consequences of their actions. This perspective allows them to remain calm and composed in difficult situations, to avoid impulsive decisions, and to act with deliberation and foresight.

Perspective in wisdom involves recognizing the transient nature of many of life's challenges and understanding that time often brings clarity and resolution. Wise individuals are able to take a step back from the immediacy of a situation, to consider the broader implications of their actions, and to make decisions that are informed by a deep understanding of the interconnectedness of all things. This ability to see the bigger picture allows wise individuals to act with patience, deliberation, and clarity, even in the face of uncertainty.

Balancing Conflicting Values and Priorities

Wisdom also includes the ability to balance conflicting values and priorities. Life is full of complex situations where there are no easy answers, where different values may come into conflict, and where difficult trade-offs must be made. Wisdom involves the capacity to navigate these dilemmas with nuance and sensitivity, finding a path that honors multiple perspectives and minimizes harm. This balancing act requires both intellectual rigor and emotional intelligence, as well as the courage to make difficult decisions in the face of uncertainty.

Balancing conflicting values involves recognizing the complexity of life and understanding that there are often no clear-cut answers. Wise individuals are able to hold multiple perspectives in mind, to weigh the pros and cons of different options, and to make decisions that are informed by a deep understanding of the ethical and practical implications of their actions. This ability to balance conflicting values is what allows wise individuals to navigate life's challenges with grace and integrity.

Inner Peace and Contentment

Furthermore, wisdom is often associated with a sense of inner peace and contentment. Wise individuals tend to be less driven by external validation or material success and more focused on inner fulfillment and living in accordance with their values. They understand that true happiness comes from within and that it is found in living a life of purpose, integrity, and connection with others. This inner peace allows them to approach life with a sense of calm and equanimity, even in the face of challenges and adversity.

Inner peace in wisdom is the result of living a life that is aligned with one's values and priorities. Wise individuals understand that true fulfillment comes from within and that it is found in living a life that is meaningful, purposeful, and connected to others. This sense of inner peace allows wise individuals to approach life's challenges with a sense of calm and assurance, knowing that they are living in accordance with their values and contributing to the greater good.

The Collective Aspects of Wisdom

Wisdom also involves the ability to learn from others. Wise individuals are not isolated in their knowledge; they seek out the counsel and insights of others, recognizing that everyone has something to teach. They are open to different perspectives and are willing to incorporate the wisdom of others into their own understanding. This collaborative approach to wisdom enriches their own insights and helps them to make more informed and balanced decisions.

Learning from others is an essential component of wisdom, as it allows individuals to broaden their understanding and to see things from multiple perspectives. Wise individuals are able to draw on the collective wisdom of their community, seeking out the insights and experiences of others to inform their own decisions. This collaborative approach to wisdom not only enriches their own understanding but also fosters a sense of connection and community as they recognize the value of the insights and experiences of others.

Wisdom as a Lifelong Pursuit

Wisdom is a lifelong pursuit. It is not something that is achieved once and for all, but a quality that continues to grow and deepen over time. As individuals encounter new experiences, face new challenges, and engage in ongoing reflection, their wisdom expands and evolves. This continual growth is part of what makes wisdom such a valuable and enduring quality; it is a source of guidance and strength that can be relied upon throughout life's many twists and turns.

Wisdom is a dynamic and evolving quality, one that is shaped by the experiences and reflections of a lifetime. It is a journey, not a destination, and it requires ongoing effort, reflection, and growth. Wise individuals understand that there is always more to learn and that wisdom is not a static trait but a process of continuous development. This commitment to lifelong learning is what allows wise individuals to navigate life's challenges with grace and insight and to contribute positively to the world around them.

The Enduring Value of Wisdom

In conclusion, wisdom is a virtue that spans deep understanding, sound judgment, compassion, humility, and perspective, embodying a holistic approach to grasping the intricacies of life and human behavior. It is born from experience, nurtured through reflection, and guided by ethical principles. Wisdom allows individuals to navigate the complexities of life with grace and insight, to make decisions that are both effective and aligned with their values, and to contribute positively to the world around them. It is a quality that enriches both the individual and the community, leading to a more meaningful, fulfilled, and harmonious life.

Wisdom is not just about making good decisions; it is about living a life that is aligned with one's values and priorities and that contributes positively to the world. It is a quality that allows individuals to navigate life's challenges with grace and integrity, to learn from their experiences, and to grow and develop over time. By cultivating wisdom, individuals can create a life that is rich in meaning, purpose, and fulfillment and that is a source of guidance and strength throughout life's many twists and turns.

CHAPTER 13
RESILIENCE

"The greatest glory in living lies not in never falling, but in rising every time we fall." — Nelson Mandela

Resilience: The Strength to Endure and Thrive

Resilience is a vital and transformative quality that enables individuals to adapt to adversity, recover from setbacks, and thrive despite challenges. It encompasses the capacity to withstand and bounce back from difficult situations, demonstrating strength and flexibility in the face of stress, trauma, or change. Resilience is not just about enduring hardship but about emerging from it with renewed strength and perspective, making it a crucial attribute for personal growth and success.

The Core Components of Resilience

At its core, resilience is the ability to maintain psychological and emotional stability amid adversity. It involves several key components, including adaptability, perseverance, and optimism. Adaptability refers to the capacity to adjust to new conditions and changes, allowing individuals to cope with unexpected events and navigate through them effectively. Perseverance is the determination to keep moving forward despite obstacles and setbacks. Optimism, or the tendency to maintain a positive outlook, helps individuals envision a better future and remain motivated to overcome difficulties.

The Role of Mindset in Resilience

One of the essential aspects of resilience is its connection to mindset. A resilient mindset is characterized by the belief that challenges can be overcome and that individuals have the resources and abilities to manage difficulties. This mindset, often referred to as a growth mindset, contrasts with a fixed mindset, which views challenges as threats and believes that abilities are static. A growth mindset fosters resilience by encouraging individuals to see setbacks as opportunities for learning and growth rather than as insurmountable failures.

Individuals with a growth mindset approach challenges with curiosity and a willingness to learn, understanding that failures are not permanent but rather stepping stones to success. This perspective empowers them to persevere through difficulties, continuously improving and adapting. By embracing a growth mindset, individuals can cultivate resilience, enabling them to tackle challenges with confidence and an open mind.

Emotional Regulation and Its Importance

Resilience is also deeply rooted in emotional regulation. The ability to manage and process emotions effectively is crucial for maintaining stability during times of stress. Resilient individuals are able to experience their emotions without being overwhelmed by them. They can acknowledge and accept their feelings, but they do not let these emotions dictate their actions or cloud their judgment. Emotional regulation helps individuals to remain calm under pressure, make rational decisions, and maintain a sense of balance even in challenging situations.

Effective emotional regulation involves recognizing and understanding one's emotions, accepting them as natural responses to external events, and finding constructive ways to cope with them. This skill enables individuals to navigate through difficult emotions such as fear, anger, or sadness without being consumed by them. By maintaining emotional balance, resilient individuals can approach problems with clarity and composure, making informed decisions that lead to positive outcomes.

The Power of Social Support

Another critical component of resilience is social support. The presence of a strong support network, including family, friends, and colleagues, plays a significant role in enhancing resilience. Social support provides emotional comfort, practical assistance, and a sense of connection, all of which are crucial for navigating adversity. Resilient individuals often have close relationships with others who offer encouragement, guidance, and a listening ear. These relationships can serve as a source of strength and reassurance, helping individuals to feel less isolated and more capable of facing challenges.

Social support not only offers immediate relief during difficult times but also contributes to long-term resilience. Knowing that there are people who care and are willing to help creates a sense of security and belonging. This connection to others fosters resilience by reinforcing the belief that one is not alone in facing challenges and that there are resources available to assist in overcoming obstacles.

Self-Efficacy and Resilience

Resilience is also linked to self-efficacy, which is the belief in one's ability to influence and control events in one's life. Individuals with high self-efficacy are more likely to approach challenges with confidence and persistence, believing that their actions can make a difference. This sense of agency and control is empowering and reinforces resilience by encouraging individuals to take proactive steps to address difficulties and to persist in their efforts despite setbacks.

Self-efficacy fosters a proactive approach to problem-solving, enabling individuals to set goals, take action, and adapt strategies as needed. This belief in one's own abilities boosts confidence and motivation, making it easier to tackle challenges head-on. By cultivating self-efficacy, individuals can strengthen their resilience, enhancing their ability to navigate adversity and achieve their goals.

The Role of Purpose and Direction

Furthermore, resilience involves having a sense of purpose and direction. A clear sense of purpose provides motivation and helps individuals to stay focused on their goals, even in the face of adversity. It gives meaning to their efforts and helps them to persevere through difficult times. Resilient individuals often have a strong sense of what they want to achieve and a commitment to their values and goals, which helps them to remain determined and resilient when facing obstacles.

Having a sense of purpose acts as an anchor during turbulent times, providing a stable foundation upon which to build resilience. This purpose-driven approach to life helps individuals to maintain their focus and motivation, even when circumstances are challenging. By staying connected to their values and long-term goals, resilient individuals can navigate adversity with determination and grace, emerging stronger and more focused on what truly matters.

Building and Strengthening Resilience

Resilience is not a fixed attribute but a capacity that can be cultivated and enhanced over time. While some people may naturally exhibit higher levels of resilience, it is also a quality that can be cultivated through intentional effort and practice. Building resilience involves developing coping strategies, such as problem-solving skills, stress management techniques, and positive thinking habits. Engaging in activities that promote well-being, such as regular exercise, mindfulness practices, and maintaining healthy relationships, can also enhance resilience.

Developing resilience requires a commitment to personal growth and self-care. By practicing stress management techniques, individuals can reduce the negative impact of stress on their physical and emotional health. Engaging in regular physical activity, maintaining a balanced diet, and getting enough sleep are all essential components of resilience, as they provide the energy and mental clarity needed to cope with challenges.

Mindfulness practices, such as meditation and deep breathing exercises, can also enhance resilience by helping individuals to stay grounded in the present moment and to approach challenges with a calm and focused mind. By cultivating these habits, individuals can strengthen their resilience and improve their overall well-being, enabling them to navigate life's challenges with greater ease and confidence.

Learning from Adversity

Experiencing adversity and overcoming challenges can also contribute to the development of resilience. Each encounter with difficulty provides an opportunity to learn, adapt, and grow. Resilient individuals often reflect on their experiences, gaining insights and developing strategies that help them to handle future challenges more effectively. This process of learning from adversity and applying those lessons contributes to a greater sense of resilience and confidence.

Adversity can be a powerful teacher, offering valuable lessons about one's strengths, weaknesses, and capacity for growth. By reflecting on past challenges and identifying the strategies that were effective in overcoming them, individuals can build a toolkit of resilience that will serve them well in future situations. This process of learning and growth not only enhances resilience but also fosters a sense of empowerment and self-efficacy as individuals come to recognize their ability to navigate adversity successfully.

Resilience at the Organizational and Community Levels

In addition to personal resilience, organizational and community resilience are also important. Organizations and communities that foster resilience are better equipped to handle disruptions, adapt to changes, and support their members through difficult times. Building resilience at these levels involves creating supportive environments, promoting collaboration, and developing systems and structures that enhance the capacity to respond to challenges effectively.

Organizational resilience involves creating a culture that values adaptability, innovation, and continuous improvement. By fostering a supportive and inclusive environment, organizations can help their members to develop the skills and mindset needed to navigate change and adversity. This includes providing opportunities for professional development, encouraging open communication, and promoting work-life balance.

Community resilience, on the other hand, involves strengthening social networks, fostering a sense of belonging, and building systems that support the well-being of all members. This can include creating community programs that provide resources and support during times of crisis, promoting social cohesion, and encouraging collaboration and mutual aid. By building resilient communities, individuals are better able to cope with challenges and contribute to the well-being of others.

Resilience in the Face of Global Challenges

In the context of global challenges, such as climate change, pandemics, and social inequality, resilience becomes a critical factor in our collective ability to adapt and thrive. Communities, organizations, and governments must develop resilient systems and strategies to address these complex issues effectively. This involves not only responding to immediate crises but also planning for long-term sustainability and resilience.

For instance, building resilient communities might involve developing infrastructure that can withstand natural disasters, creating social support networks that help individuals and families cope with economic hardship, and fostering a culture of collaboration and mutual support. On a broader scale, resilient societies are those that can adapt to changing circumstances, innovate in the face of adversity, and work collectively to overcome challenges. Resilience as a Lifelong Journey

Resilience is not a fixed trait but a dynamic process that evolves over time. It is a lifelong journey of growth, adaptation, and learning. As individuals encounter new challenges and experiences, their resilience is tested and strengthened. This continuous process of development is what makes resilience such a valuable and enduring quality. It is a source of strength that can be relied upon throughout life's many twists and turns.

Resilience is a journey that requires ongoing effort and commitment. It involves continuously learning from experiences, reflecting on one's growth, and adapting to new circumstances. By embracing this journey, individuals can cultivate a deep and enduring sense of resilience that will serve them well throughout their lives.

The Benefits of Resilience

The benefits of resilience extend far beyond the ability to cope with adversity. Resilient individuals tend to experience higher levels of well-being, greater life satisfaction, and stronger relationships. They are better equipped to handle stress, adapt to change, and maintain a positive outlook even in the face of challenges. Resilience also fosters a sense of empowerment and self-efficacy, as individuals come to recognize their capacity to navigate adversity and achieve their goals.

Resilience not only enhances individual well-being but also contributes to the well-being of others. Resilient individuals are often able to provide support and encouragement to those around them, helping others to navigate challenges and build their own resilience. This ripple effect of resilience can have a profound impact on families, communities, and organizations, creating a culture of strength, adaptability, and mutual support.

The Essence of Resiliency

In conclusion, resiliency is a vital quality that allows individuals to navigate life's challenges with strength, adaptability, and perseverance. It involves maintaining a positive outlook, managing emotions effectively, adapting to change, and having a sense of purpose. Support systems, personal practices, and a growth mindset all contribute to building and strengthening resilience. By developing these attributes and skills, individuals can enhance their ability to cope with adversity and to thrive in the face of challenges.

Resiliency is not just about enduring hardship but about thriving despite it, finding ways to grow and succeed even in the most difficult circumstances. It is a dynamic and evolving quality that can be cultivated and strengthened over time, allowing individuals and communities to navigate the unpredictable nature of life with confidence and grace. As we continue to face the challenges and uncertainties of life, the development of resilience will remain essential for personal fulfillment, collective well-being, and the pursuit of a meaningful and purposeful life.

CHAPTER 14
EMPATHY

"Too often we underestimate the power of a touch, a smile, a kind word, a listening ear, an honest compliment, or the smallest act of caring, all of which have the potential to turn a life around." — Leo Buscaglia

Empathy: The Heartbeat of Human Connection

Empathy is an essential quality that enables individuals to understand, share, and connect with the emotions and experiences of others. It is the capacity to perceive and relate to the feelings, thoughts, and perspectives of another person, fostering deeper connections and enhancing interpersonal relationships. Empathy goes beyond mere sympathy or pity; it involves a genuine effort to grasp another's emotional state and to respond with compassion and understanding. It is a cornerstone of effective communication, meaningful relationships, and social harmony.

Cognitive and Emotional Empathy: Two Sides of the Same Coin

At its core, empathy involves two main components: cognitive empathy and emotional empathy. Cognitive empathy refers to the ability to recognize and understand another person's thoughts, feelings, and perspectives. It involves putting oneself in someone else's shoes and comprehending their experiences from their point of view. This type of empathy is crucial for effective communication, as it allows individuals to grasp the underlying emotions and motivations behind others 'words and actions.

Emotional empathy, on the other hand, is the ability to actually feel or experience the emotions of another person. It involves an emotional resonance with someone else's feelings, such as feeling joy when they are happy or sadness when they are distressed. Emotional empathy helps individuals to connect on a deeper level, fostering a sense of shared experience and mutual understanding. This emotional connection is essential for building trust and nurturing supportive relationships.

While cognitive empathy enables us to intellectually understand another person's situation, emotional empathy allows us to share in their feelings. Together, these two forms of empathy create a holistic understanding of others, enabling us to respond with both compassion and insight. This dual capacity is what makes empathy such a powerful tool in building connections and fostering understanding between people.

Empathy as the Foundation of Strong Relationships

One of the key benefits of empathy is its role in fostering strong and meaningful relationships. When individuals practice empathy, they are better able to connect with others, build trust, and establish rapport. Empathetic interactions create a sense of validation and support, making individuals feel heard and understood. This validation is crucial for emotional well-being and contributes to healthier and more satisfying relationships, whether in personal or professional contexts.

Empathy allows us to see beyond our own perspectives and to appreciate the feelings and experiences of others. This understanding fosters a sense of connection and intimacy, which are the cornerstones of any strong relationship. By practicing empathy, we can create deeper bonds with those around us, enhancing the quality of our interactions and the strength of our relationships.

Empathy in Conflict Resolution and Problem-Solving

Empathy also plays a significant role in conflict resolution and problem-solving. When individuals approach conflicts with empathy, they are more likely to understand the underlying issues and perspectives of all parties involved. This understanding facilitates more constructive dialogue, helps to identify common ground, and enables the development of mutually beneficial solutions. Empathy promotes a collaborative approach to resolving conflicts, reducing hostility, and fostering a positive and respectful environment.

In conflict situations, empathy allows us to step back from our own emotions and viewpoints and to consider the feelings and needs of others. This perspective shift can diffuse tension and open the door to more productive conversations. By acknowledging and validating the emotions of others, empathetic individuals can create a space where all parties feel heard and respected, paving the way for resolution and healing.

Empathy as a Pillar of Effective Leadership and Teamwork

In addition to its impact on relationships and conflict resolution, empathy is a critical component of effective leadership and teamwork. Empathetic leaders are able to connect with their team members, understand their needs and concerns, and provide support and guidance. This empathetic approach enhances team cohesion, motivates individuals, and creates a positive work environment. Leaders who practice empathy are also better equipped to recognize and address issues related to employee well-being, performance, and satisfaction.

Empathy in leadership goes beyond simply understanding the needs of team members; it involves actively supporting and empowering them to succeed. Empathetic leaders create an inclusive and supportive work environment where individuals feel valued and respected. This fosters trust, loyalty, and a sense of belonging, which are essential for effective teamwork and organizational success.

The Link Between Empathy and Emotional Intelligence

Empathy is also closely linked to emotional intelligence, which is the ability to recognize, understand, and manage one's own emotions and the emotions of others. Emotional intelligence encompasses self-awareness, self-regulation, motivation, empathy, and social skills. Empathetic individuals are typically high in emotional intelligence, as they possess the ability to navigate complex social interactions, manage their own emotions, and respond appropriately to the emotions of others.

Emotional intelligence and empathy are interconnected, with each reinforcing and enhancing the other. By developing emotional intelligence, individuals can improve their empathetic abilities, enabling them to connect more deeply with others and to navigate social interactions with greater ease and effectiveness. This emotional intelligence is crucial for building strong relationships, resolving conflicts, and leading with compassion and understanding.

Developing and Practicing Empathy

Developing and practicing empathy involves several key strategies. Active listening is one of the most important techniques for enhancing empathy. Active listening involves giving full attention to the speaker, acknowledging their emotions, and responding thoughtfully. By actively listening, individuals demonstrate that they value the other person's perspective and are genuinely interested in understanding their experiences.

Active listening requires more than just hearing the words being spoken; it involves paying attention to non-verbal cues, such as body language and tone of voice, that can provide deeper insight into the speaker's emotions and intentions. By engaging in active listening, individuals can develop a more nuanced understanding of others, fostering empathy and strengthening their relationships.

Another strategy for developing empathy is practicing mindfulness. Mindfulness involves being fully present in the moment and paying attention to one's own thoughts, feelings, and sensations without judgment. Mindfulness can help individuals become more aware of their own emotional responses and more attuned to the emotions of others. This heightened awareness enhances the ability to empathize and respond compassionately.

Mindfulness also encourages a non-judgmental approach to understanding others, allowing individuals to accept and appreciate different perspectives and experiences without rushing to judgment. This open-mindedness is essential for cultivating empathy, as it enables individuals to connect with others on a deeper level and to respond with kindness and understanding.

Additionally, seeking diverse perspectives and experiences can enrich one's understanding and empathy. By exposing oneself to different cultures, backgrounds, and viewpoints, individuals can broaden their understanding of the human experience and develop a greater appreciation for the challenges and experiences of others. Engaging with diverse perspectives fosters empathy by highlighting the commonalities and differences in human experiences.

Exposure to diverse perspectives can challenge preconceived notions and expand one's worldview, leading to a more empathetic and inclusive approach to others. By actively seeking out and engaging with different perspectives, individuals can develop a deeper understanding of the complexities of human experience and enhance their capacity for empathy.

Empathy in Social Justice and Advocacy

Empathy is also a crucial aspect of social justice and advocacy. Understanding and empathizing with the experiences of marginalized and oppressed groups can drive efforts to address inequalities and promote social change. Empathetic advocacy involves listening to the voices of those who are affected by injustice, amplifying their concerns, and working towards solutions that address their needs and rights.

Empathy in social justice requires a willingness to listen and learn from those who have been marginalized and to use that understanding to advocate for meaningful change. It involves recognizing the systemic barriers that contribute to inequality and working to dismantle them in a way that is inclusive and equitable. By cultivating empathy, individuals can become more effective advocates for social justice, promoting a more just and compassionate society.

Challenges to Practicing Empathy

Despite its many benefits, empathy can sometimes be challenging to practice. Factors such as stress, cognitive biases, and personal experiences can affect one's ability to empathize. For example, individuals may struggle to empathize with those who have different values or beliefs, or they may find it difficult to connect with others when they are overwhelmed by their own emotions. Developing empathy requires intentional effort, self-awareness, and a commitment to understanding and supporting others, even in challenging situations.

Cognitive biases, such as the tendency to favor those who are similar to us or to judge others based on stereotypes, can hinder our ability to empathize with those who are different from us. Overcoming these biases requires conscious effort and a willingness to challenge our own assumptions and prejudices. By practicing self-awareness and actively working to overcome cognitive biases, individuals can develop a more empathetic and inclusive approach to others.

Personal stress and emotional overload can also impact one's ability to empathize. When individuals are overwhelmed by their own emotions, it can be difficult to focus on the needs and feelings of others. Developing healthy coping mechanisms and stress management strategies can help individuals maintain their empathy, even in difficult circumstances.

Empathy as a Fundamental Quality for Personal and Professional Success

Empathy is a fundamental quality that enhances human connections, fosters effective communication and contributes to personal and professional success. It involves both cognitive and emotional components, allowing individuals to understand and share the experiences and emotions of others. Empathy strengthens relationships, aids in conflict resolution, and is crucial for effective leadership and teamwork.

By practicing active listening, mindfulness, and seeking diverse perspectives, individuals can develop and enhance their empathetic abilities. These practices not only foster empathy but also contribute to overall well-being, as they encourage deeper connections, greater understanding, and a more compassionate approach to others.

Empathy as a Force for Positive Change

Ultimately, empathy is a powerful force for creating positive change, promoting social justice, and building a more compassionate and understanding world. It enables us to connect with others on a deeper level, to understand their experiences and perspectives, and to respond with kindness and compassion. In a world that is often divided by differences, empathy has the power to bring people together, to bridge gaps, and to foster a sense of shared humanity.

Empathy is not just a personal quality; it is a social force that can transform communities and societies. By cultivating empathy in ourselves and encouraging it in others, we can create a more inclusive, compassionate, and just world. Empathy is the foundation of social harmony, and it is through empathy that we can build a world where everyone is valued, respected, and understood.

The Enduring Value of Empathy

In conclusion, empathy allows individuals to connect with others on a deep and meaningful level. It involves both cognitive and emotional components, allowing us to understand and share in the experiences and emotions of others. Empathy is crucial for building strong relationships, resolving conflicts, and leading with compassion and understanding. By practicing empathy, we can enhance our emotional intelligence, foster social harmony, and create a more just and compassionate world.

Empathy is not just about understanding others; it is about connecting with them on a human level, recognizing our shared experiences and emotions, and responding with kindness and compassion. By cultivating empathy in our daily lives, we can build stronger relationships, promote social justice, and contribute to a more inclusive and understanding world. Empathy is the heartbeat of human connection, and it is through empathy that we can create a world where everyone is seen, heard, and valued.

CHAPTER 15
FORGIVENESS

"The weak can never forgive. Forgiveness is the attribute of the strong." — Mahatma Gandhi

The Power and Process of Forgiveness

Forgiveness centers around the process of letting go of resentment, anger, and the desire for retribution towards someone who has caused harm or offense. It is a deeply personal and often challenging journey that can lead to emotional healing, improved relationships, and a greater sense of inner peace. Forgiveness is not about condoning or excusing harmful behavior but about releasing the hold that negative emotions have on one's well-being and moving forward with a renewed sense of freedom and compassion.

Understanding Forgiveness: An Act of Empathy and Understanding

At its core, forgiveness is an act of empathy and understanding. It involves recognizing the humanity and imperfections of others, acknowledging that everyone makes mistakes and that nobody is beyond redemption. By choosing to forgive, individuals allow themselves to see beyond the wrongdoing, focusing instead on the broader context of the person's life and their own emotional needs. This shift in perspective helps to break the cycle of blame and bitterness, creating space for healing and reconciliation.

Forgiveness requires the ability to understand and empathize with the person who has caused harm. This does not mean excusing their behavior, but rather recognizing that they, too, are human with their own struggles and imperfections. By viewing the situation through this empathetic lens, individuals can begin to detach themselves from the negative emotions associated with the harm and move towards a place of understanding and compassion.

Forgiveness Misunderstood: Strength in Vulnerability

Forgiveness is often misunderstood as a sign of weakness or as an act that requires forgetting the past. In reality, forgiveness is a powerful and courageous act that requires strength, self-awareness, and emotional resilience. It does not mean forgetting or condoning the behavior, nor does it necessarily involve reconciliation with the person who caused harm. Instead, forgiveness is about freeing oneself from the grip of negative emotions and choosing to move forward with a sense of peace and acceptance.

Choosing to forgive is not about ignoring or diminishing the pain that was caused. Rather, it is about acknowledging that pain and deciding not to let it define one's emotional landscape. This decision requires vulnerability, as it involves confronting and processing difficult emotions. However, it is through this vulnerability that individuals find the strength to release those emotions and reclaim their sense of well-being.

The Health Benefits of Forgiveness

One of the key benefits of forgiveness is its impact on emotional and physical health. Holding onto anger, resentment, and grudges can have detrimental effects on one's mental and physical well-being. Chronic stress, anxiety, and depression are often linked to unresolved conflicts and unaddressed emotional pain. Forgiveness, by contrast, has been shown to reduce stress levels, lower blood pressure, and improve overall emotional health. It allows individuals to release the burden of negative emotions and to experience greater emotional balance and resilience.

The act of forgiving can trigger physiological changes in the body, such as reducing cortisol levels, the hormone associated with stress. This reduction in stress hormones can lead to improvements in immune function, cardiovascular health, and overall longevity.

By letting go of negative emotions, individuals can experience a sense of relief and liberation, which contributes to both mental and physical health.

Forgiveness and Relationship Healing

Forgiveness also plays a crucial role in improving relationships and fostering social harmony. When individuals choose to forgive, they are able to repair and strengthen relationships that may have been damaged by conflict or misunderstanding. Forgiveness can pave the way for open communication, mutual understanding, and a renewed sense of trust and connection. It creates an opportunity for healing and growth, allowing individuals to move past grievances and build stronger, more supportive relationships.

In relationships, whether personal or professional, conflicts are inevitable. However, the ability to forgive can transform these conflicts into opportunities for deeper connection and understanding. By choosing to forgive, individuals demonstrate their commitment to the relationship and their willingness to prioritize harmony over discord. This act of forgiveness can lead to a more resilient and trusting relationship where both parties feel valued and understood.

The Process of Forgiveness

The process of forgiveness often involves several stages, including acknowledging the hurt, processing emotions, and making a conscious decision to forgive. Acknowledging the hurt is an important first step, as it involves recognizing and validating the impact of the wrongdoing. This acknowledgment helps to confront and address the emotional pain rather than suppressing or ignoring it.

Acknowledging the hurt requires honesty and self-reflection. It involves recognizing the specific ways in which the harm has affected one's emotions, thoughts, and behaviors. This step is crucial because it allows individuals to fully understand the extent of their pain and to begin the process of healing.

Processing emotions involves working through feelings of anger, sadness, and betrayal in a constructive manner. This may involve seeking support from friends, family, or a therapist, as well as engaging in self-care practices that promote emotional well-being. It is important to allow oneself to experience and express these emotions, as this process is essential for healing and moving forward.

Processing emotions is not about dwelling on the pain but about finding healthy ways to express and release it. This may involve talking about the experience with a trusted confidant, journaling, or engaging in creative outlets such as art or music. By processing these emotions, individuals can begin to let go of the negative energy associated with the harm and move towards a place of healing.

Making a conscious decision to forgive is a critical step in the forgiveness process. This decision involves a deliberate choice to let go of resentment and to adopt a more compassionate and understanding perspective. It is an act of personal empowerment that allows individuals to reclaim control over their emotional state and to move forward with a sense of peace and acceptance.

The decision to forgive is often accompanied by a sense of relief and liberation. It is the moment when individuals choose to prioritize their own well-being over the desire for retribution or justice. This decision is not always easy, but it is a powerful step towards healing and emotional freedom.

Challenges and Complexities of Forgiveness

Forgiveness can be particularly challenging when the harm caused is severe or when the person who caused the harm has not expressed remorse or sought reconciliation. In such cases, forgiveness may involve a process of inner work and self-reflection rather than a direct interaction with the person who caused harm. It is important to recognize that forgiveness is ultimately about personal healing and emotional freedom rather than about the actions or responses of others.

Forgiving someone who has not shown remorse or who continues to cause harm can be one of the most difficult challenges in the forgiveness process. In these situations, forgiveness may not involve reconciliation or continued contact with the person who caused harm. Instead, it becomes a deeply personal journey of letting go of negative emotions and reclaiming one's sense of peace.

There are also cultural and individual variations in the way forgiveness is understood and practiced. Different cultures and belief systems may have unique perspectives on forgiveness, and individual experiences and values can influence one's approach to this process. It is important to approach forgiveness in a way that aligns with one's personal values and beliefs while also being open to the possibility of growth and healing.

Cultural beliefs and societal norms can shape how individuals perceive and practice forgiveness. In some cultures, forgiveness may be seen as a necessary step for restoring harmony and maintaining social cohesion. In others, forgiveness may be viewed as a personal choice that reflects one's values and moral principles. Understanding these cultural influences can help individuals navigate their own forgiveness journey in a way that is authentic and meaningful.

Forgiveness as an Ongoing Process

Forgiveness is not a one-time event but an ongoing process that may require repeated effort and reflection. It involves continually choosing to let go of negative emotions and to embrace a more compassionate and understanding perspective. This ongoing process requires patience, self-compassion, and a commitment to personal growth.

The journey of forgiveness is often non-linear, with moments of progress and setbacks. It is common for individuals to experience lingering feelings of anger or resentment, even after they have made the decision to forgive. This is why forgiveness must be seen as an ongoing practice, one that requires regular reflection and reaffirmation of the choice to let go and move forward.

Self-compassion plays a vital role in this ongoing process. Forgiving oneself for struggling with forgiveness is essential. Understanding that it is okay to experience mixed emotions and that forgiveness is a journey rather than a destination can help individuals stay committed to the process.

The Transformative Power of Forgiveness

Forgiveness is a powerful and transformative act that involves letting go of resentment and anger, and choosing to move forward with a sense of peace and acceptance. It is a process that requires strength, self-awareness, and emotional resilience, and it has significant benefits for emotional and physical health, as well as for improving relationships. Forgiveness involves acknowledging the hurt, processing emotions, and making a conscious decision to let go of negative emotions. It is an ongoing process that may vary based on cultural and individual perspectives, but its core essence remains the same: the pursuit of personal healing and emotional freedom.

By embracing forgiveness, individuals can experience greater emotional balance, improved relationships, and a renewed sense of inner peace and well-being. The act of forgiving, whether it is of others or oneself, is a testament to the human capacity for growth, empathy, and transformation. It is a courageous act that frees the heart from the chains of resentment and opens the door to a life of greater harmony and fulfillment.

Forgiveness and Personal Growth

Forgiveness is deeply intertwined with personal growth. Through the process of forgiving, individuals often discover new aspects of themselves, including their capacity for empathy, compassion, and understanding. This journey of self-discovery can lead to a greater sense of self-awareness and emotional maturity.

Personal growth through forgiveness involves reflecting on the lessons learned from the experience and using those insights to make positive changes in one's life. It may involve setting healthier boundaries, developing stronger communication skills, or cultivating a more compassionate outlook on life. As individuals grow through the process of forgiveness, they often find themselves more resilient and better equipped to handle future challenges.

Forgiveness in the Context of Self-Forgiveness

While forgiveness is often thought of in terms of forgiving others, self-forgiveness is equally important. Self-forgiveness involves letting go of guilt, shame, and self-blame for past mistakes or failures. It is a process of accepting one's imperfections and recognizing that everyone is capable of growth and change.

Self-forgiveness requires the same steps as forgiving others: acknowledging the hurt, processing emotions, and making a conscious decision to let go of negative feelings. However, it also involves cultivating self-compassion and understanding that making mistakes is a natural part of the human experience. By forgiving oneself, individuals can release the burden of self-judgment and move forward with greater self-acceptance and peace.

Embracing Forgiveness for a Fulfilled Life

In conclusion, forgiveness is a complex, multifaceted process that encompasses empathy, understanding, emotional resilience, and personal growth. It is not about excusing harmful behavior but about freeing oneself from the weight of negative emotions and choosing to live with peace and compassion. Forgiveness has profound benefits for emotional and physical health, relationships, and overall well-being. It is a journey that requires ongoing effort, reflection, and a commitment to healing and growth.

By embracing forgiveness, whether towards others or oneself, individuals can cultivate a deeper sense of inner peace, improve their relationships, and experience a greater sense of fulfillment in life. Forgiveness is a powerful act of self-liberation, allowing individuals to move beyond pain and resentment and to live with greater joy, harmony, and connection.

CHAPTER 16
ETHICS

"Ethics is the activity of man directed to secure the greatest good for himself and others." — Aristotle

The Foundation of Ethics: A Guide to Moral Principles and Values

Ethics is a fundamental branch of philosophy that deals with questions of morality, examining what is right and wrong, good and bad, just and unjust. It provides a framework for making decisions that align with values and principles that are considered virtuous or morally sound. Ethics is not only a theoretical discipline but also a practical guide for living a life that is consistent with principles of justice, fairness, and respect for others. It encompasses a wide range of issues, from personal behavior and professional conduct to social justice and global responsibility.

Moral Principles: The Core of Ethical Decision-Making

At the core of ethics lies the concept of moral principles—guidelines that help individuals and societies determine what actions are permissible and what are not. These principles often include values such as honesty, integrity, fairness, and respect for others. They serve as a compass for decision-making, helping people navigate complex situations where the right course of action may not be immediately clear. Ethical principles are essential for fostering trust and cooperation in relationships, whether they are personal, professional, or communal.

Moral principles act as the foundation for ethical behavior, offering a consistent and universal approach to evaluating the morality of actions. These principles are rooted in the idea that certain actions or behaviors are inherently right or wrong, regardless of individual or cultural differences. For instance, the principle of honesty dictates that lying or deceit is morally wrong, while the principle of fairness requires treating others equitably and without bias. These guiding values shape our interactions and ensure that our actions are aligned with the broader good.

Ethics and Individual Character: The Reflection of Moral Values

One of the most important aspects of ethics is its role in shaping individual character and behavior. Ethical behavior is often seen as a reflection of one's character, as it demonstrates a commitment to living according to moral values and principles. For example, a person who consistently acts with integrity, even when no one is watching, is often regarded as ethical because they prioritize doing what is right over personal gain or convenience. This alignment between behavior and ethical principles is crucial for maintaining a sense of personal integrity and self-respect.

Ethical character is built over time through the consistent practice of moral principles. It involves making choices that are guided by values such as honesty, compassion, and justice, even in the face of temptation or adversity. Individuals with strong ethical character are often seen as trustworthy and dependable, as their actions consistently reflect their commitment to doing what is right. This trustworthiness is essential in building and maintaining relationships, whether in personal, professional, or communal contexts.

Professional Ethics: The Role of Codes of Conduct

Ethics also plays a vital role in professional life, where it is often formalized into codes of conduct or ethical guidelines. These codes serve to ensure that professionals act in ways that are consistent with the values of their profession and the expectations of society. For instance, medical ethics emphasizes the importance of patient confidentiality, informed consent, and non-maleficence (the principle of not causing harm). Similarly, business ethics focuses on issues such as corporate social responsibility, transparency, and fair treatment of employees and customers. Adherence to professional ethics is essential for maintaining public trust and upholding the standards of the profession.

Professional ethics guide the behavior of individuals within specific fields, ensuring that their actions align with the values and expectations of their profession. These ethical guidelines help professionals navigate complex situations and make decisions that prioritize the well-being of their clients, customers, or patients. For example, in the medical field, the Hippocratic Oath serves as a guiding principle for physicians, emphasizing the importance of patient care and ethical medical practice. Similarly, in the legal profession, attorneys are bound by ethical standards that prioritize justice, fairness, and client confidentiality.

Social Ethics: Collective Responsibilities and Social Justice

In addition to individual and professional ethics, there is also a broader societal dimension to ethics, which concerns the collective responsibilities of individuals and groups toward each other and the environment. Social ethics addresses issues such as justice, equality, and human rights, seeking to create a society that is fair and just for all its members. This aspect of ethics is particularly important in addressing systemic inequalities and injustices that affect marginalized or vulnerable populations. It involves questioning and challenging social norms and structures that perpetuate discrimination, exploitation, and oppression.

Social ethics is concerned with the broader impact of our actions on society as a whole. It involves recognizing the interconnectedness of individuals within a community and understanding the collective responsibilities that we have toward one another. This includes advocating for social justice, promoting equality, and working to address systemic issues that contribute to inequality and injustice. Social ethics calls for a commitment to creating a society that values and respects the dignity and rights of all individuals, regardless of their background or circumstances.

Environmental Ethics: Expanding Moral Consideration to the Natural World

Environmental ethics, a relatively recent development in the field, extends ethical considerations to the natural world. It examines the moral relationship between humans and the environment, emphasizing the need for sustainable practices that protect ecosystems and preserve biodiversity. Environmental ethics challenges the notion of human dominion over nature, advocating instead for a more harmonious and respectful relationship with the planet. This branch of ethics is critical in addressing the global environmental crises we face today, such as climate change, deforestation, and pollution.

Environmental ethics expands the scope of moral consideration beyond human beings to include the natural world. It recognizes the intrinsic value of nature and the importance of preserving the environment for future generations. This ethical perspective challenges the traditional view of humans as separate from and superior to nature, instead advocating for a more holistic approach that considers the well-being of all living beings and the planet as a whole. Environmental ethics calls for a commitment to sustainable practices, conservation efforts, and environmental stewardship to protect and preserve the natural world.

The Intersection of Ethics and Law: Guiding Moral Judgment

Ethics also intersects with law, although the two are not synonymous. While laws are formal rules enacted by governments to regulate behavior, ethics is concerned with the moral principles that should guide behavior, whether or not these principles are codified in law. Laws can be unethical, as seen in historical examples of legal systems that permitted slavery, discrimination, or genocide. Conversely, ethical behavior can sometimes require civil disobedience or resistance to unjust laws. Thus, ethics provides a higher standard by which laws and legal systems can be evaluated and critiqued.

The relationship between ethics and law is complex and multifaceted. While laws are designed to regulate behavior and maintain social order, they do not always align with ethical principles. In some cases, laws may be unjust or discriminatory, and ethical considerations may call for resistance or reform. For example, during the Civil Rights Movement in the United States, individuals engaged in acts of civil disobedience to challenge unjust laws and promote social justice. This demonstrates the importance of ethics as a guiding force for evaluating and critiquing legal systems and advocating for change.

Ethical Relativism vs. Ethical Universalism: Navigating Cultural Differences

One of the challenges of ethics is its subjective nature—what is considered ethical can vary greatly depending on cultural, religious, and personal beliefs. Ethical relativism, the idea that there are no absolute moral truths and that ethics is relative to the norms of a particular culture or society, reflects this diversity. However, this perspective can lead to moral uncertainty or the belief that all ethical views are equally valid, which complicates efforts to establish universal ethical standards.

Ethical relativism recognizes the diversity of moral beliefs and practices across different cultures and societies. It suggests that what is considered right or wrong is determined by cultural norms and values and that there are no objective or universal moral standards. This perspective challenges the idea of absolute morality and emphasizes the importance of understanding and respecting cultural differences. However, ethical relativism also raises questions about the possibility of moral progress and the ability to critique harmful or oppressive practices within different cultures.

In contrast, ethical universalism posits that there are certain moral principles that are universally applicable, regardless of cultural differences. This perspective is often associated with human rights, which are seen as inherent to all individuals by virtue of their humanity. The Universal Declaration of Human Rights, adopted by the United Nations in 1948, is an example of an attempt to establish a global standard for ethics that transcends cultural and national boundaries.

Ethical universalism asserts that there are fundamental moral principles that apply to all people, regardless of their cultural or social context. This perspective emphasizes the inherent dignity and rights of all individuals and seeks to establish universal ethical standards that promote justice, equality, and human flourishing. Ethical universalism provides a framework for addressing global challenges and advocating for the protection of human rights on a global scale.

The Evolving Nature of Ethics: Adapting to a Changing World

Despite the challenges, ethics remains a vital and dynamic field that continues to evolve as society changes. New ethical dilemmas arise with advances in technology, changes in social norms, and the increasing interconnectedness of the global community. Issues such as privacy in the digital age, artificial intelligence, and global inequality require ongoing ethical reflection and debate.

The evolving nature of ethics reflects the complexity of the modern world and the need for continuous adaptation and reflection. As new technologies emerge and social norms shift, ethical considerations must be reexamined and reevaluated to address new challenges and opportunities. For example, the rise of social media and digital communication has raised ethical questions about privacy, consent, and the impact of technology on human relationships. Similarly, advances in artificial intelligence and biotechnology have prompted debates about the ethical implications of these technologies and their potential impact on society.

Ethics must also grapple with global challenges such as climate change, poverty, and inequality. These issues require a collective response that is guided by ethical principles such as justice, fairness, and sustainability. Ethical reflection and debate are essential for developing solutions that are not only effective but also aligned with the values and principles that promote the common good.

Ethical Decision-Making: Balancing Principles and Pragmatism

Ethical decision-making involves balancing moral principles with practical considerations. It requires individuals to navigate complex situations where there may be competing values or conflicting interests. Ethical decision-making often involves a process of reflection, analysis, and dialogue, where individuals consider the potential consequences of their actions, the impact on others, and the alignment with their moral values.

One approach to ethical decision-making is the principle-based approach, which emphasizes the importance of adhering to moral principles such as honesty, fairness, and respect for others. This approach provides a clear framework for evaluating the morality of actions and decisions, but it may not always provide definitive answers in complex situations.

Another approach is the consequentialist approach, which focuses on the outcomes or consequences of actions. This approach emphasizes the importance of considering the impact of decisions on the well-being of others and the overall good. Consequentialist ethics is often associated with utilitarianism, which advocates for actions that maximize overall happiness or well-being.

Ethical decision-making also involves the consideration of context and the unique circumstances of each situation. This requires individuals to be flexible and open-minded, recognizing that ethical dilemmas often involve shades of gray rather than clear-cut answers. Ethical decision-making is a process of continuous learning and reflection, where individuals strive to make decisions that are aligned with their values and principles while also being mindful of the complexities and nuances of each situation.

The Role of Education in Ethics

Education plays a crucial role in fostering ethical awareness and understanding. Ethical education involves teaching individuals about moral principles, values, and ethical frameworks, as well as developing critical thinking skills and ethical reasoning. By providing individuals with the tools to navigate ethical dilemmas and make informed decisions, ethical education helps to cultivate a sense of moral responsibility and integrity.

Ethical education can take place in a variety of settings, from formal academic institutions to informal community programs. It can be integrated into various subjects and disciplines, including philosophy, social studies, science, and business. Ethical education encourages individuals to engage in reflective and critical thinking, to consider the impact of their actions on others, and to develop a commitment to ethical behavior in all aspects of life.

In addition to formal education, ethical awareness can also be fostered through experiential learning and real-world experiences. For example, service-learning programs, internships, and volunteer opportunities provide individuals with the chance to engage with ethical issues in a practical and hands-on way. These experiences help to deepen understanding and provide valuable insights into the complexities of ethical decision-making.

Ethics in the Global Context: Challenges and Opportunities

In the increasingly interconnected world, ethics must be considered on a global scale. Issues such as climate change, global inequality, and human rights violations transcend national boundaries and require a collective ethical response. Global ethics emphasizes the need for cooperation and collaboration among nations and cultures to address these shared challenges.

Global ethics involves recognizing the interconnectedness of individuals and communities around the world and understanding the impact of our actions on a global scale. It calls for a commitment to social justice, human rights, and environmental sustainability, and it challenges us to think beyond our own immediate interests to consider the well-being of the global community.

Global ethics also presents opportunities for cross-cultural dialogue and learning. By engaging with diverse perspectives and cultural traditions, individuals can develop a more nuanced and inclusive understanding of ethics. This cross-cultural engagement fosters mutual respect and understanding, and it helps to build bridges between different communities and cultures.

The Future of Ethics: Emerging Challenges and Continuing Relevance

As we look to the future, ethics will continue to play a vital role in shaping the direction of society. Emerging challenges such as the ethical implications of artificial intelligence, the impact of technology on privacy and human relationships, and the ongoing struggle for social justice and equality will require ongoing ethical reflection and debate.

Ethics will also continue to be relevant in addressing the environmental challenges that we face. The ethical imperative to protect the planet and preserve the natural world for future generations will remain a central concern as we navigate the complexities of climate change and environmental degradation.

The future of ethics will also involve a continued commitment to education and the development of ethical awareness. As new generations emerge, it will be essential to provide them with the tools and knowledge to navigate the ethical challenges of their time.

This will require a commitment to fostering critical thinking, ethical reasoning, and a deep understanding of moral principles and values.

Ethics as a Moral Compass

In conclusion, ethics is an intricate and layered discipline that guides individuals and societies in making decisions that align with moral principles and values. It encompasses personal integrity, professional conduct, social justice, and environmental responsibility. While ethical beliefs may vary across cultures and contexts, the pursuit of ethics remains central to the quest for a just and equitable world. As we navigate the challenges of the modern world, ethics provides the moral compass that helps us strive for fairness, compassion, and respect for all beings.

Ethics challenges us to think deeply about our actions and their impact on others, and it calls us to live in a way that is consistent with our values and principles. It is a discipline that is both deeply personal and profoundly social, shaping the way we interact with others and the world around us. By embracing ethics as a guiding force in our lives, we can create a more just, compassionate, and sustainable world for ourselves and future generations.

CHAPTER 17
SACRIFICE

"The important thing is this: to be able at any moment to sacrifice what we are for what we could become." — Charles Du Bos

Sacrifice: A Profound and Multifaceted Concept in Human Experience

Sacrifice is a nuanced concept deeply engrained into the human experience. At its core, sacrifice involves giving up something valuable for the sake of something greater, whether that be a cause, a person, or a higher principle. This willingness to relinquish personal gain in favor of a larger good is often viewed as a noble act that reflects the depth of human compassion, courage, and commitment.

Sacrifice in Personal Relationships: A Testament to Love and Commitment

In personal relationships, sacrifice often manifests as an expression of love and commitment. Parents frequently make significant personal sacrifices to ensure the well-being and success of their children. This could involve financial sacrifices, such as saving and investing in their children's education, or personal sacrifices, such as spending long hours away from home to provide a better life for their family. Such acts, though sometimes challenging, are driven by the deep love and desire to nurture the next generation. This personal sacrifice is not always recognized or celebrated, but it forms the backbone of many familial and social structures.

The sacrifices made within families and close relationships are often the most profound and impactful, as they are rooted in the deep bonds of love, trust, and responsibility. These sacrifices can take many forms, from the everyday compromises made in a marriage to the more significant sacrifices of career opportunities or personal time to care for a loved one in need.

The notion of sacrifice in personal relationships also extends to friendships and partnerships, where individuals may give up their own comfort or convenience to support or stand by their friends and partners during difficult times. This willingness to prioritize the needs and well-being of others over one's own desires is a testament to the strength and depth of human connection.

However, the concept of sacrifice in relationships must be approached with care and balance. While selflessness is a virtue, it is important to recognize that sacrifice should not lead to self-neglect or enable unhealthy dynamics. In healthy relationships, sacrifice is reciprocal and grounded in mutual respect, ensuring that both parties feel valued and supported.

Leadership and Sacrifice: Serving the Greater Good

The concept of sacrifice is also prevalent in leadership and public service. Leaders often make sacrifices to serve their communities, nations, or organizations. This could mean sacrificing personal time, comfort, or even safety for the greater good. For example, during times of crisis or conflict, leaders may put their own needs aside to address the needs of their people. This kind of sacrifice requires a strong sense of purpose and commitment and often serves as a powerful example of dedication and selflessness.

Sacrifice in leadership is not only about giving up personal gains but also about making difficult decisions that prioritize the welfare of others over one's own interests. True leadership involves a commitment to the values of integrity, justice, and service, even when it comes at a personal cost.

Historical figures such as Mahatma Gandhi, Nelson Mandela, and John F. Kennedy exemplify the concept of sacrificial leadership. These leaders made tremendous personal sacrifices, including enduring imprisonment, persecution, and even death, in their pursuit of justice, equality, and freedom for their people. Their willingness to sacrifice for the greater good has left a lasting legacy and continues to inspire future generations of leaders.

In contemporary contexts, sacrificial leadership is seen in various forms, from political leaders who advocate for the marginalized to corporate leaders who prioritize ethical practices over profits. These leaders recognize that true success is not measured by personal gain, but by the positive impact they have on the lives of others and the world.

The Complexities and Risks of Sacrifice

Sacrifice, however, is not without its complexities and potential pitfalls. It can sometimes lead to negative consequences if not balanced with self-care and personal well-being. The concept of self-sacrifice can become problematic when it leads to neglect of one's own needs or health. The idea of giving until it hurts can result in burnout, resentment, or even harm if one's sacrifices are not made thoughtfully. It is crucial to recognize that true sacrifice should ideally come from a place of balance and mindful consideration rather than compulsion or self-neglect.

In professional settings, for example, the expectation of sacrifice can sometimes lead to unhealthy work environments where employees are expected to prioritize work over personal life, leading to stress and burnout. While dedication to one's work is commendable, it is essential to maintain a balance that allows for personal well-being and fulfillment.

In relationships, the idea of sacrifice can sometimes be manipulated or taken advantage of, leading to imbalanced dynamics where one person consistently sacrifices more than the other. This can result in feelings of resentment, exhaustion, and emotional depletion. It is important to recognize the boundaries of healthy sacrifice and to ensure that it is mutually appreciated and reciprocated.

Sacrifice must be approached with mindfulness and an understanding of its limits. It is essential to recognize that self-care is not selfishness, and that maintaining one's own well-being is necessary to continue supporting others effectively. Sacrifice should be an empowering choice rather than a burden, made with the awareness of its impact on oneself and others.

Sacrifice and Social Justice: The Pursuit of Equality

In societal contexts, sacrifice can also be viewed through the lens of social justice and equality. Many individuals and movements have sacrificed personal comfort and safety to fight for broader social change. Activists and reformers often put their own lives on the line to challenge injustices and advocate for the rights of others. These sacrifices, while personal, contribute to a larger narrative of progress and equity. The legacy of such sacrifices can inspire future generations to continue the work towards a more just and equitable world.

The Civil Rights Movement in the United States, for example, is a powerful testament to the sacrifices made by individuals who stood up against racial injustice. Figures like Rosa Parks, who faced arrest and persecution for refusing to give up her seat on a segregated bus, and the thousands of unnamed activists who risked their lives to march for equality, exemplify the courage and commitment required to challenge systemic oppression.

Similarly, the fight for gender equality has been marked by the sacrifices of countless women and men who have advocated for the rights of women and marginalized genders. The suffragette movement, which fought for women's right to vote, and the ongoing struggle for gender parity in the workplace and beyond, are fueled by the sacrifices of those who refuse to accept injustice.

These sacrifices are not only about personal risk but also about the willingness to confront societal norms and structures that perpetuate inequality. The act of sacrifice in the pursuit of social justice is a powerful statement of one's commitment to the belief that all individuals deserve equal rights and opportunities.

Sacrifice as a Catalyst for Solidarity and Community

Moreover, the act of sacrifice can foster a sense of solidarity and communal strength. When individuals make sacrifices for the benefit of others, it can create a ripple effect of goodwill and cooperation. This collective effort often leads to a more cohesive and resilient community, where mutual support and shared values enhance overall well-being and progress.

In times of crisis, such as natural disasters or pandemics, the willingness of individuals to sacrifice personal comfort and resources for the greater good becomes evident. Communities come together to provide support, share resources, and care for the most vulnerable members. This sense of solidarity is a powerful force that strengthens the social fabric and fosters a spirit of collective responsibility.

Sacrifice in the context of community also involves the willingness to contribute time, effort, and resources to communal projects and initiatives. Whether it is volunteering for a local charity, participating in community clean-up efforts, or supporting local businesses, these acts of sacrifice contribute to the overall well-being and prosperity of the community.

The collective sacrifices made by individuals within a community often lead to a sense of shared purpose and identity. This sense of belonging and connection is essential for building strong, resilient communities that can withstand challenges and thrive together.

The Ethical Dimensions of Sacrifice

At its heart, sacrifice is a testament to the human spirit's capacity for empathy, love, and selflessness. It underscores the idea that personal gain is not the sole measure of success or fulfillment. Instead, the act of giving up something of value for a greater cause reflects a deep understanding of interconnectedness and shared responsibility. Sacrifice highlights the ability to transcend individual desires in favor of contributing to a larger, collective good.

The ethical dimensions of sacrifice raise important questions about the motivations and consequences of sacrificial acts. Is the sacrifice made out of genuine altruism, or is it driven by the expectation of recognition or reward? Is the sacrifice voluntary, or is it coerced by societal pressures or expectations? These questions are crucial for understanding the true nature of sacrifice and its impact on individuals and society.

Ethical considerations also come into play when evaluating the consequences of sacrifice. While sacrifice can lead to positive outcomes, it can also result in unintended negative consequences. For example, the sacrifice of environmental resources for economic development may lead to short-term gains but long-term ecological damage. Similarly, the sacrifice of personal well-being for the sake of career advancement may lead to professional success but at the cost of mental and physical health.

It is important to approach sacrifice with a critical and reflective mindset, considering the broader implications and consequences of sacrificial acts. True sacrifice should be guided by ethical principles that prioritize the well-being of individuals and the collective good.

Sacrifice and Personal Growth: The Path to Self-Realization

Sacrifice is also closely linked to personal growth and self-realization. The act of giving up something valuable often requires individuals to confront their own fears, attachments, and limitations.

This process of letting go can lead to profound personal transformation and a deeper understanding of oneself.

In many spiritual traditions, sacrifice is seen as a path to enlightenment or self-realization. By renouncing material possessions, ego-driven desires, or worldly attachments, individuals can cultivate inner peace, clarity, and a deeper connection with their true selves. This process of self-sacrifice is not about self-denial but about transcending the ego and realizing one's higher potential.

In everyday life, the sacrifices we make often lead to personal growth and development. Whether it is sacrificing short-term pleasures for long-term goals, giving up unhealthy habits for a healthier lifestyle, or letting go of toxic relationships to create space for positive connections, these acts of sacrifice contribute to our overall well-being and fulfillment.

The journey of sacrifice is often accompanied by moments of struggle and doubt, but it is through these challenges that individuals discover their inner strength and resilience. Sacrifice teaches us the value of patience, perseverance, and the ability to prioritize what truly matters in life.

Sacrifice in the Global Context: Collective Responsibility and Action

In the global context, sacrifice takes on a broader significance, encompassing collective responsibility and action. As the world becomes increasingly interconnected, the challenges we face, such as climate change, global inequality, and pandemics, require a collective response that involves sacrifices from individuals, communities, and nations.

The global environmental movement, for example, calls for sacrifices in terms of lifestyle changes, consumption patterns, and resource use to protect the planet for future generations. These sacrifices are necessary to mitigate the impact of climate change, preserve biodiversity, and ensure a sustainable future. The willingness to make these sacrifices reflects a commitment to the well-being of the planet and the recognition that our actions have far-reaching consequences.

Similarly, the fight against global inequality and poverty requires sacrifices in terms of economic resources, political will, and social change. Addressing these issues involves a collective effort to redistribute wealth, provide access to education and healthcare, and create opportunities for all individuals to thrive. The sacrifices made in this context are driven by a sense of global justice and the belief in the inherent dignity and rights of all people.

The COVID-19 pandemic has also highlighted the importance of collective sacrifice in the face of global challenges. The sacrifices made by healthcare workers, essential workers, and individuals who adhered to public health measures reflect a commitment to protecting the most vulnerable members of society and mitigating the spread of the virus. These sacrifices have been essential in navigating the crisis and working towards recovery.

The Enduring Power of Sacrifice

Sacrifice is a powerful concept that plays a crucial role in shaping personal relationships, leadership, social justice, and communal solidarity. While it comes with its challenges and potential risks, the essence of sacrifice lies in its capacity to reflect profound human virtues and contribute to the greater good. By embracing sacrifice with a thoughtful and balanced approach, individuals and communities can foster a sense of purpose, compassion, and shared responsibility that enriches the human experience and drives positive change.

Sacrifice is not merely about giving up something valuable; it is about making a conscious choice to prioritize the well-being of others and the collective good. It is a testament to the strength of the human spirit and the depth of our capacity for empathy, love, and selflessness. In a world that often emphasizes individualism and personal gain, sacrifice reminds us of the importance of connection, community, and the greater good.

As we navigate the complexities of the modern world, the concept of sacrifice will continue to be relevant and essential. It challenges us to think beyond ourselves, to consider the impact of our actions on others, and to strive for a more just, compassionate, and sustainable world. By embracing sacrifice as a guiding principle, we can create a future where the well-being of all individuals and the planet is prioritized and where the values of empathy, love, and selflessness are at the heart of our collective efforts.

CHAPTER 18
FAITH

"**Faith is taking the first step even when you don't see the whole staircase.**" — **Martin Luther King Jr.**

Faith: A Journey Beyond Belief

Faith is an intrinsic element of the human experience, a guiding light in the darkness, and a source of strength in times of uncertainty. It is more than a belief system; it is a journey, a deep and abiding trust in something greater than ourselves. Whether rooted in religious traditions or personal spirituality, faith has the power to shape our lives, influence our decisions, and connect us to the divine.

The Timeless Journey of Faith

The journey of faith is one that transcends time and place. It is a path walked by countless souls throughout history, each seeking meaning, purpose, and connection with the transcendent. In every culture and civilization, faith has played a pivotal role in shaping human consciousness, providing answers to the profound questions of existence, and offering solace in the face of life's inevitable challenges.

Throughout history, faith has been a guiding force in both personal and collective experiences. Ancient civilizations looked to their gods and spiritual practices to explain natural phenomena, to guide their communities, and to provide a moral framework for living. Whether in the temples of ancient Greece, the ziggurats of Mesopotamia, or the pyramids of Egypt, faith was central to understanding the mysteries of the universe and human existence.

Faith is often born in the quiet moments of introspection, where the soul reaches out to the unknown, yearning for understanding and peace. It is in these moments of stillness that we come to realize the limitations of our human understanding and the vastness of the universe. Faith begins where knowledge ends, where the mysteries of life invite us to trust in the unseen and the unknowable.

Religious Traditions and the Framework of Faith

For many, faith is rooted in religious traditions passed down through generations. These traditions offer a framework for understanding the world, providing sacred texts, rituals, and practices that guide believers on their spiritual journey. In Christianity, for example, faith is central to the teachings of Jesus Christ, who called on his followers to trust in God's plan and to live according to divine principles. The Bible, sacraments, and the communal worship experience all serve as vehicles for nurturing and expressing faith.

Similarly, in Islam, faith, or "iman," is one of the Five Pillars, serving as the foundation of a Muslim's life and relationship with Allah. Muslims are called to submit to the will of Allah, demonstrating their faith through prayer, fasting, charity, and pilgrimage. The Quran and Hadith provide the moral and spiritual guidance necessary to live a life of faith, while the practice of daily prayers (Salah) fosters a continual connection with the divine.

In Hinduism, faith is expressed through devotion to the various deities and adherence to dharma, the moral and ethical code that governs one's actions. The Bhagavad Gita, Vedas, and Upanishads are some of the sacred texts that provide guidance for living a life in harmony with the divine order. Rituals such as puja (worship), meditation, and the recitation of mantras are expressions of faith that connect the individual with the cosmic principles that underlie existence.

Buddhism, although often considered more of a philosophy than a traditional religion, also emphasizes faith—faith in the Buddha, the Dharma (teachings), and the Sangha (community). This faith is not blind belief but is based on personal experience and the inner conviction that the path of enlightenment is achievable. Through practices such as meditation, mindfulness, and ethical living, Buddhists cultivate a faith that is grounded in wisdom and compassion.

Personal Spirituality and Faith

Faith is not confined to organized religion. Many people find their spiritual path outside traditional religious institutions, drawing on personal experiences, nature, and the inner voice of conscience to guide them. This form of faith is deeply personal and often involves a quest for self-discovery and inner peace. It is a faith that is not bound by dogma or doctrine but is instead an ongoing exploration of the divine as it manifests in everyday life.

Personal spirituality allows individuals to define their own relationship with the divine, free from the constraints of formalized religion. This can include a belief in a higher power, the search for meaning in life, or a commitment to living in accordance with one's deepest values and principles. Practices such as meditation, yoga, nature walks, journaling, or simply quiet contemplation can become sacred rituals that nurture this personal faith.

For some, personal spirituality is inspired by nature's beauty and complexity. The grandeur of mountains, the serenity of oceans, and the intricate patterns of life all evoke a sense of awe and wonder, pointing to a reality beyond what we can see and touch. This connection to the natural world fosters a faith that is grounded in the rhythms and cycles of life, reflecting the deep interconnection between all living beings.

Others may find faith through acts of service and compassion, seeing the divine in the faces of those they help and the communities they uplift. This type of faith is often action-oriented, expressed through a commitment to social justice, environmental stewardship, or humanitarian work. It is a faith that sees the sacred in the every day and seeks to bring about a more just and loving world.

The Challenges and Growth of Faith

The journey of faith is rarely straightforward. It is often marked by trials, doubts, and moments of crisis. These challenges are not signs of weakness but rather opportunities for growth and deepening understanding. In times of hardship, faith becomes a refuge, a source of hope and resilience that sustains us through the darkest nights. It is during these times that faith is tested, revealing its true strength and power.

Doubt is a natural companion on the journey of faith. It is through questioning and seeking that our faith is refined and strengthened. Doubt pushes us to explore the depths of our beliefs, to confront our fears and uncertainties, and to seek answers that resonate with our deepest convictions. Far from being the opposite of faith, doubt is an integral part of the spiritual journey, a catalyst for growth and transformation.

Moments of doubt and crisis often lead to a deeper, more mature faith. When faced with life's inevitable difficulties—whether it be loss, illness, or existential uncertainty—individuals are challenged to reassess their beliefs and find new ways of understanding their relationship with the divine. This process can lead to a more nuanced and resilient faith, one that is not shaken by adversity but is instead strengthened by it.

For some, these challenges may lead to a reevaluation of their faith, resulting in a shift away from traditional religious practices towards a more personal and individualized spirituality. Others may find that their trials deepen their commitment to their religious community and its teachings, reinforcing the bonds of faith and fellowship. Regardless of the path, these experiences contribute to the richness and complexity of the journey of faith.

Faith as a Source of Connection

Faith is also a source of profound connection—to the divine, to others, and to ourselves. It unites people across cultures, languages, and traditions, creating a sense of shared purpose and belonging. Through faith, we come to understand our place in the universe and our relationship with the greater whole. It teaches us compassion, empathy, and the importance of community, reminding us that we are all interconnected.

Religious communities often serve as the heart of this connection, providing a space for believers to come together, share their faith, and support one another. Whether it is through communal worship, study groups, or social gatherings, these communities offer a sense of belonging and a shared journey towards spiritual growth. The bonds formed within these communities are often deep and enduring, grounded in a mutual commitment to living out the values and teachings of their faith.

Interfaith dialogue and cooperation further demonstrate the unifying power of faith. In a world often divided by differences, faith can serve as a bridge, fostering understanding and collaboration across religious and cultural boundaries. Initiatives that bring together people of different faiths to work towards common goals—such as peace, justice, and environmental sustainability—highlight the potential for faith to be a force for unity and positive change.

On a personal level, faith fosters a connection with the self, encouraging introspection and self-awareness. It invites individuals to explore their innermost thoughts, desires, and fears, providing a framework for personal growth and transformation. Through practices such as prayer, meditation, or reflective reading, faith helps individuals cultivate a deeper understanding of themselves and their purpose in life.

The Act of Surrender in Faith

At its core, faith is an act of surrender. It is the willingness to let go of control, to trust in the unfolding of life's events, and to believe in a higher purpose, even when it is not immediately apparent. This surrender is not a sign of defeat but a recognition of the limits of human understanding and the boundless wisdom of the divine. It is through this surrender that we find peace, knowing that we are held in the hands of something greater than ourselves.

Surrender in faith involves accepting that not everything can be understood or controlled by human reason. It is an acknowledgment that life is full of uncertainties and that there is a greater plan at work, even if it is beyond our comprehension. This surrender allows individuals to let go of the need for certainty and to embrace the mystery of existence, trusting that there is meaning and purpose even in the unknown.

This act of surrender can be deeply liberating. By releasing the need to control every aspect of life, individuals open themselves to the possibility of experiencing life more fully and authentically. It allows for a greater sense of openness and receptivity to the experiences, lessons, and opportunities that life presents, fostering a sense of peace and acceptance.

Faith as a Lifelong Journey

The journey of faith is ongoing, a lifelong process of learning, growing, and evolving. It is not a destination to be reached but a path to be walked with humility, openness, and trust. Along the way, we may encounter challenges, moments of doubt, and periods of darkness, but it is through these experiences that our faith is deepened and enriched.

Faith is dynamic and ever-changing, reflecting the ebb and flow of life itself. It evolves as individuals grow and change, adapting to new experiences, insights, and challenges. This continuous process of growth and transformation ensures that faith remains relevant and vital throughout one's life.

As individuals move through different stages of life, their faith may take on new meanings and dimensions. For example, the faith of a young person may be characterized by a sense of idealism and exploration, while the faith of an older adult may be marked by a deeper sense of wisdom, acceptance, and surrender. Each stage of life offers new opportunities for deepening one's faith and for discovering new aspects of the divine.

Faith also calls for ongoing engagement and practice. Whether through regular prayer, meditation, study, or service to others, the practice of faith requires commitment and dedication. It is through these practices that faith is nurtured and sustained, allowing individuals to stay connected to the divine and to continue growing in their spiritual journey.

Faith as a Gift

In the end, faith is a gift—an invitation to see beyond the material world, to connect with the divine, and to live a life of purpose, meaning, and love. It can lead us through the uncertainties of life, illuminating our path and offering hope in the face of the unknown.

Faith provides a sense of hope and assurance, even in the face of life's greatest challenges. It reminds us that we are not alone, that there is a greater purpose to our existence, and that we are part of something much larger than ourselves. This sense of connection and purpose gives life meaning and direction, guiding us through both the joys and sorrows of life.

Ultimately, faith is an expression of the human spirit's deepest longings and aspirations. It is a reflection of our desire for connection, understanding, and transcendence. Whether expressed through religious practice, personal spirituality, or acts of compassion and service, faith is a powerful force that shapes our lives and our world.

In a world often marked by uncertainty and change, faith offers a steady and enduring source of strength and guidance. It calls us to trust in the unseen, to believe in the possibilities that lie beyond our immediate understanding, and to live with courage, compassion, and love. Faith is a journey, a quest that leads us deeper into the mysteries of life and the wonders of the universe.

CHAPTER 19
PATIENCE

"Have patience with all things, but first of all with yourself."

— François de Sales

Patience: A Timeless Virtue and Path to Enduring Strength

Patience is a timeless virtue that subtly influences the human experience. It is the quiet strength that sustains us in times of adversity, the gentle endurance that guides us through life's trials, and the steadfast resolve that helps us achieve our long-term goals. In a world increasingly characterized by immediacy and instant gratification, patience remains a rare and invaluable quality, one that requires deliberate practice and mindful cultivation.

The Essence of Patience

At its essence, patience is the ability to endure delay, discomfort, or suffering without becoming frustrated or agitated. It is the capacity to wait with a calm and positive attitude, trusting that things will unfold in their own time. This virtue is not merely about enduring the passage of time but involves a deeper understanding and acceptance of the natural rhythms of life. Patience teaches us to navigate life's inevitable ebbs and flows with grace, to embrace uncertainty, and to find peace in the present moment.

Patience is more than just waiting; it is how we behave while we wait. It is about maintaining composure, sustaining a hopeful outlook, and continuing to put forth effort even when immediate results are not visible. This quality of patience is deeply interwoven with other virtues such as faith, resilience, and compassion. It requires a balance between striving towards goals and accepting the current moment, understanding that every stage of life has its own pace and timing.

Patience in Personal Development

Patience is not a passive state of waiting but an active engagement with the present moment. It requires a conscious choice to remain steadfast in the face of challenges, to respond with grace and understanding when faced with delays or difficulties. This active patience is grounded in a deep sense of purpose and an unwavering belief that the journey, with all its ups and downs, is meaningful and valuable.

In the realm of personal development, patience plays a crucial role in achieving long-term goals and cultivating resilience. The process of growth, whether in personal skills, relationships, or professional endeavors, often involves setbacks, periods of stagnation, and moments of doubt. Patience provides the endurance needed to persevere through these challenges, allowing us to stay focused on our objectives and maintain a positive outlook.

The Role of Patience in Achieving Goals

The achievement of significant goals is often a long and arduous process. Whether learning a new skill, building a career, or developing a meaningful relationship, the journey is rarely straightforward. It requires continuous effort, adaptability, and the ability to withstand the frustrations that come with obstacles and delays. Patience enables us to keep our eyes on the bigger picture, to stay motivated even when progress is slow, and to remain committed to our goals despite temporary setbacks.

In the world of education and skill development, for example, patience is essential. The process of learning is incremental, and mastery comes only through sustained effort over time. Whether it's learning to play a musical instrument, acquiring a new language, or developing expertise in a professional field, the path to success is often long and filled with challenges. Patience allows us to appreciate the gradual improvements and to stay engaged in the learning process, knowing that each step forward brings us closer to our goal.

Patience in Relationships

The practice of patience also enhances our relationships with others. It enables us to approach interactions with empathy and understanding, recognizing that everyone has their own pace and struggles. In moments of conflict or misunderstanding, patience allows us to listen with an open heart, to respond thoughtfully rather than react impulsively. It fosters a sense of respect and compassion, creating a space where genuine connection and resolution can flourish.

In romantic relationships, patience is vital for building trust and intimacy. Relationships require time to grow and evolve, and patience allows partners to navigate the inevitable ups and downs with grace. It helps individuals to give each other the space to grow, to understand and accept each other's flaws, and to work through differences without resorting to anger or frustration.

In friendships and family relationships, patience is equally important. It helps us to be present for our loved ones, to offer support without judgment, and to accept them as they are. Patience also allows us to weather the storms that can arise in close relationships, such as disagreements, misunderstandings, or periods of distance. By practicing patience, we create an environment where relationships can deepen and flourish over time.

Patience in Leadership and Professional Life

In leadership and professional life, patience is a key attribute that contributes to effective decision-making and the ability to guide others through challenges. Leaders who demonstrate patience are able to think strategically, consider different perspectives, and make informed decisions without rushing to conclusions. This quality is especially important in situations that require navigating uncertainty or managing conflicts.

Patience in leadership also involves the ability to nurture and develop talent within a team or organization. Recognizing that growth takes time, patient leaders provide the support and resources needed for individuals to develop their skills and reach their potential. This approach fosters a positive work environment where employees feel valued and motivated, leading to greater collaboration and long-term success.

In the professional sphere, patience is also critical when dealing with complex projects or navigating career advancement. The path to success is rarely linear, and setbacks or delays are common. Patience allows professionals to stay focused on their long-term goals, to persist through challenges, and to maintain a positive attitude even in the face of obstacles. It also enables them to build meaningful professional relationships and to navigate workplace dynamics with grace and composure.

The Challenges of Cultivating Patience

However, the journey of cultivating patience is not without its difficulties. It often requires us to confront our own impatience and discomfort, to acknowledge and address the underlying fears and anxieties that drive our desire for immediate results. Patience demands a willingness to let go of control and to trust in the process, even when the outcome is uncertain. This can be a challenging endeavor, requiring ongoing self-reflection and mindfulness.

In today's fast-paced world, where instant gratification is often the norm, practicing patience can be particularly challenging. The constant exposure to rapid information, quick results, and immediate feedback can create an expectation for instant success or resolution. This environment can make it difficult to tolerate delays or to engage in long-term projects that require sustained effort and dedication.

To cultivate patience, it is essential to develop strategies that help manage impatience and frustration. These may include mindfulness practices, such as meditation or deep breathing, which help to calm the mind and bring awareness to the present moment. Engaging in activities that require focus and attention, such as gardening, crafting, or long-distance running, can also help to develop patience by teaching the value of gradual progress and the rewards of persistence.

Patience and the Transformation of Time

One of the most profound aspects of patience is its ability to transform our experience of time. Rather than seeing time as a series of obstacles to be overcome or deadlines to be met, patience invites us to embrace the present moment and appreciate the journey. It encourages us to find meaning and fulfillment in the process rather than fixating solely on the end result.

When we cultivate patience, we shift our focus from the destination to the journey itself. This shift allows us to experience life more fully, to savor the small moments of joy and accomplishment that occur along the way. It helps us to appreciate the beauty and richness of each moment, rather than constantly striving for the next goal or achievement.

Patience also changes our relationship with time by fostering a sense of trust in the natural flow of life. It teaches us to let go of the need to control every outcome and to accept that things will unfold in their own time. This acceptance brings a sense of peace and contentment, allowing us to live in harmony with the rhythms of life rather than resisting them.

Patience in the Broader Societal Context

In a broader societal context, patience also has the power to foster social harmony and collective progress. The challenges facing our world, from social justice issues to environmental concerns, often require sustained effort and collaboration. Patience allows us to engage in these efforts with a long-term perspective, recognizing that meaningful change takes time and persistence. It inspires us to work together with empathy and understanding, to build a more compassionate and equitable world.

The pursuit of social justice, for example, is often a long and arduous process. Efforts to address systemic inequalities, protect human rights, and create a more just society require patience and perseverance. Social change does not happen overnight; it involves ongoing advocacy, education, and collaboration. Patience in this context means continuing to fight for justice even when progress is slow or setbacks occur. It also involves the patience to listen to others 'experiences, to build coalitions, and to engage in dialogue that fosters mutual understanding and respect.

Similarly, the environmental movement requires a long-term commitment to sustainability and conservation. The challenges of climate change, biodiversity loss, and resource depletion cannot be solved with quick fixes. They require sustained effort, patience, and the willingness to make sacrifices for the benefit of future generations. Patience in this context involves understanding the long-term impacts of our actions, making choices that prioritize the health of the planet, and working collaboratively to create a sustainable future.

Patience as Inner Strength and Resilience

In essence, patience is a reflection of our inner strength and resilience. It is a testament to our ability to endure, to trust in the unfolding of life, and to find peace in the midst of uncertainty. It is a virtue that enriches our lives, deepens our connections with others, and enhances our capacity for growth and transformation.

Patience is a source of inner strength because it allows us to remain centered and grounded in the face of adversity. It helps us to maintain our composure and clarity of mind, even when circumstances are challenging or unpredictable. This inner strength enables us to navigate life's ups and downs with grace, to stay true to our values, and to persevere through difficult times.

Patience also contributes to resilience by helping us to recover from setbacks and to continue moving forward. It allows us to view challenges as opportunities for growth rather than as insurmountable obstacles. This mindset of patience and resilience enables us to bounce back from failures, to learn from our experiences, and to keep striving towards our goals.

The Practice of Cultivating Patience

As we embark on the journey of exploring patience, may we come to understand its profound significance and its transformative power. May we learn to cultivate patience within ourselves, to approach life's challenges with grace and endurance, and to embrace the beauty and wisdom that emerge from the quiet virtue of waiting. In doing so, we may discover a deeper sense of fulfillment and connection and find ourselves better equipped to navigate the complexities of life with poise and purpose.

The practice of cultivating patience requires ongoing self-awareness and intentionality. It involves recognizing the moments when impatience arises and choosing to respond with patience instead. This practice can be supported by mindfulness techniques, such as meditation or deep breathing, which help to bring awareness to the present moment and to calm the mind.

Engaging in activities that require focus and persistence can also help to develop patience. Whether it's practicing a musical instrument, tending to a garden, or working on a long-term project, these activities teach the value of gradual progress and the rewards of sustained effort.

It is also important to cultivate patience in our interactions with others. This involves practicing active listening, responding with empathy and understanding, and allowing others the space to express themselves at their own pace. By approaching relationships with patience, we create an environment of trust and respect, where genuine connection and mutual understanding can flourish.

The Enduring Power of Patience

Patience is a timeless virtue that enriches our lives, deepens our relationships, and enhances our capacity for growth and transformation. It is a quiet strength that sustains us through life's challenges, a gentle endurance that guides us towards our goals, and a steadfast resolve that fosters resilience and inner peace.

In a world that often prioritizes immediacy and instant gratification, the practice of patience offers a powerful antidote. It teaches us to slow down, to appreciate the present moment, and to trust in the natural rhythms of life. It encourages us to approach challenges with grace and perseverance, to cultivate empathy and understanding in our relationships, and to engage in the long-term work of creating a more just and compassionate world.

As we cultivate patience within ourselves, we discover a deeper sense of fulfillment and connection, and we become better equipped to navigate the complexities of life with poise and purpose. Patience is not merely about waiting; it is about how we wait, how we engage with the present moment, and how we approach the journey of life with an open heart and a steady spirit. Through patience, we find the strength to endure, the wisdom to grow, and the grace to embrace the beauty of life's unfolding.

CHAPTER 20
LEADERSHIP

"Leadership is not about being in charge. It is about taking care of those in your charge." — Simon Sinek

Leadership: A Journey of Vision, Service, and Growth

Leadership transcends titles or positions; it is a complex quality that shapes individuals, organizations, and entire societies. At its core, leadership is about guiding others towards a common goal, inspiring them to achieve their best, and fostering an environment where growth and innovation can thrive. It is a practice that combines vision, integrity, empathy, and resilience, and it is as much about serving others as it is about steering them.

The Essence of Leadership

The essence of leadership lies in the ability to inspire and motivate. True leaders are not merely those who hold authority but those who ignite a sense of purpose and commitment in those around them. They have a vision that goes beyond the immediate and the tangible, seeking to create a future that reflects their values and aspirations. This vision is not imposed from above but shared, communicated with clarity, and embraced by others who are inspired by the leader's passion and conviction.

A vision is more than just a goal; it is a guiding star that gives direction and meaning to the efforts of a group or organization. Leaders with a clear and compelling vision can align their team's efforts towards a common purpose, creating a sense of unity and shared endeavor. This vision must be grounded in reality, but it should also challenge and stretch the capabilities of those involved, encouraging innovation and progress.

Leadership and Service

Leadership is deeply intertwined with the concept of service. A great leader understands that their role is not to command but to serve, to lift others up, and to help them realize their potential. This servant leadership approach emphasizes empathy, humility, and a commitment to the well-being of others. It is about listening to the needs and concerns of those you lead, providing support and guidance, and fostering a collaborative environment where everyone's contributions are valued.

Servant leadership is a philosophy that turns traditional leadership on its head. Instead of viewing leadership as a position of power, servant leaders see it as a responsibility to serve others. This approach creates a culture of mutual respect and collaboration, where the leader is seen as a facilitator of success rather than a dictator of orders. By prioritizing the needs of their team members, servant leaders build trust and loyalty, which in turn fosters a more engaged and motivated workforce.

Integrity: The Cornerstone of Leadership

Integrity is a cornerstone of effective leadership. It involves consistency between one's values and actions, a commitment to ethical principles, and a dedication to honesty and transparency. Leaders who act with integrity earn the trust and respect of their followers, creating a foundation of reliability and credibility. This trust is essential for building strong relationships, overcoming challenges, and achieving collective goals.

Integrity in leadership is about doing the right thing, even when it is difficult or unpopular. It requires a commitment to ethical behavior, fairness, and accountability. Leaders who demonstrate integrity set a powerful example for others to follow, creating a culture of honesty and ethical conduct within their organization. This consistency between words and actions builds trust, which is the bedrock of any successful team or organization.

Resilience: Navigating Challenges with Strength

Resilience is another crucial aspect of leadership. The path to success is rarely smooth, and leaders often face obstacles, setbacks, and periods of uncertainty. Resilience enables leaders to navigate these challenges with composure and determination. It involves the ability to adapt to changing circumstances, to learn from failures, and to maintain focus on long-term objectives despite short-term difficulties. A resilient leader models perseverance and optimism, inspiring others to approach challenges with a similar mindset.

Resilience in leadership is about bouncing back from adversity and staying the course even when things get tough. It requires mental and emotional strength, as well as the ability to remain calm under pressure. Resilient leaders do not shy away from challenges; instead, they embrace them as opportunities for growth and learning. They encourage their teams to do the same, fostering a culture of innovation and continuous improvement.

Fostering Growth and Development

Leadership also requires the ability to foster growth and development. Great leaders are mentors and coaches, guiding others to reach their full potential. They recognize and cultivate the unique strengths of their team members, providing opportunities for learning and advancement. This commitment to personal and professional development not only enhances the capabilities of individuals but also strengthens the overall effectiveness of the team or organization.

Effective leaders understand that their success is tied to the success of their team members. They invest time and resources in developing their people, offering training, mentorship, and feedback that help individuals grow and excel. This focus on development creates a positive feedback loop, where empowered and capable team members contribute more effectively to the organization's goals, further enhancing its overall performance.

The Broader Impact of Leadership

The impact of leadership extends beyond individual interactions and organizational dynamics; it has the power to shape cultures and societies. Leaders who champion inclusivity, justice, and positive change can influence the broader social landscape, driving progress and improving lives. They are catalysts for transformation, using their influence to address pressing issues and to create a more equitable and compassionate world.

Leadership, at its best is about creating positive change, both within an organization and in the wider community. Leaders who are committed to social responsibility use their platform to advocate for justice, equality, and sustainability. They recognize that leadership is not just about achieving financial or operational success but also about making a meaningful difference in the world. This broader impact of leadership can be seen in the efforts of leaders who drive corporate social responsibility initiatives, champion diversity and inclusion, or advocate for environmental sustainability.

The Art of Communication and Connection

Effective leadership also involves the ability to communicate and connect. Leaders must be adept at conveying their vision, values, and expectations with clarity and authenticity. This involves not only speaking but also listening—truly hearing the perspectives and concerns of others. Communication is a two-way street, and leaders who engage in meaningful dialogue build stronger relationships and foster a sense of community and shared purpose.

Communication is a vital tool for leaders, as it allows them to articulate their vision and goals, align their team's efforts, and build trust and rapport. Great leaders are skilled communicators who are able to inspire and motivate others with their words. They are also active listeners, who take the time to understand the needs and concerns of their team members. This ability to connect with others on a deep level fosters collaboration and creates a sense of shared purpose and commitment.

The Continuous Journey of Leadership

The journey of leadership is both challenging and rewarding. It requires self-awareness, continuous learning, and a willingness to confront one's own limitations and biases. Leaders must be open to feedback, eager to learn from their experiences, and committed to personal growth. This journey is not a solitary one; it is a shared endeavor that involves collaboration, mutual respect, and a collective commitment to achieving common goals.

Leadership is not a destination, but a continuous journey of growth and development. Great leaders understand that they are always learning and evolving, and they actively seek out opportunities for self-improvement. They are open to feedback and willing to make changes in order to become better leaders. This commitment to personal growth is essential for staying relevant and effective in a rapidly changing world.

The Evolving Practice of Leadership

As we explore the concept of leadership, it is important to recognize that it is not a static attribute but an evolving practice. Leadership is shaped by context, culture, and the unique dynamics of each situation. It is a lifelong pursuit of excellence, characterized by an ongoing commitment to serving others, upholding ethical standards, and striving for personal and collective growth.

Leadership is a dynamic and ever-evolving practice that requires adaptability and flexibility. Great leaders are able to adjust their approach to suit the needs of the situation and the people they are leading. They understand that leadership is not a one-size-fits-all concept, and they are constantly refining their skills and strategies to stay effective. This ability to adapt and evolve is essential for navigating the complexities of modern leadership.

Leadership as a Blend of Vision, Service, Integrity, Resilience, and Growth

In essence, leadership is a blend of vision, service, integrity, resilience, and growth. It is a profound responsibility and a profound privilege, one that requires dedication, humility, and a deep understanding of the human spirit. Leaders who embody these qualities are able to inspire and guide others towards achieving their best while also making a positive impact on the world around them.

Leadership is a complex and multifaceted concept that encompasses many different qualities and attributes. It requires a deep understanding of human nature, a commitment to serving others, and the ability to inspire and motivate people to achieve their best. Great leaders are able to blend vision, service, integrity, resilience, and growth in a way that creates a positive impact on individuals, organizations, and society as a whole.

The Future of Leadership

As we look to the future, it is clear that the role of leadership will continue to evolve. The challenges of the modern world, from technological advancements to global crises, will require leaders who are adaptable, innovative, and forward-thinking. The leaders of tomorrow will need to navigate an increasingly complex and interconnected world while also addressing the pressing issues of our time, such as climate change, social inequality, and economic instability.

The future of leadership will also require a renewed focus on ethics and social responsibility. As organizations and leaders are held to higher standards of accountability, there will be a growing demand for leaders who prioritize transparency, integrity, and the well-being of all stakeholders. This shift will require leaders to adopt a more holistic and inclusive approach, one that considers the impact of their decisions on society and the environment.

The Enduring Power of Leadership

Leadership is a powerful and transformative force that has the ability to shape individuals, organizations, and societies. It is a complex and dynamic practice that requires a unique blend of vision, service, integrity, resilience, and growth. Effective leaders are able to inspire and motivate others, build trust and collaboration, and create positive change in the world.

As we continue to explore the concept of leadership, it is important to recognize that leadership is not a static attribute but an evolving practice that requires continuous learning, self-awareness, and a commitment to personal growth. Great leaders are those who are able to adapt to changing circumstances, navigate challenges with resilience, and lead with integrity and empathy.

In a world that is constantly changing and evolving, the need for effective leadership has never been greater. The leaders of tomorrow will need to be forward-thinking, innovative, and socially responsible as they navigate the complexities of the modern world. They will need to be able to inspire and motivate others while also addressing the pressing issues of our time.

Ultimately, leadership is a profound responsibility and a profound privilege. It is a journey that requires dedication, humility, and a deep understanding of the human spirit. By embracing the qualities of vision, service, integrity, resilience, and growth, leaders have the power to create positive change, inspire others, and make a lasting impact on the world around them.

CHAPTER 21
CHARACTER

"The true test of a man's character is what he does when no one is watching." — John Wooden

Character: The Foundation of Integrity, Resilience, and Empathy

Character is the bedrock upon which our lives are built, the silent force that shapes our decisions, behaviors, and interactions with others. It is the reflection of our core values, beliefs, and principles, and it fundamentally defines who we are as individuals. In a world that often emphasizes appearance, success, and external validation, character remains a profound and enduring measure of true worth. It is the compass that guides us through life's complexities, the foundation upon which we build trust and the essence of our integrity.

At its heart, character is about consistency between our values and our actions. It is the alignment of what we believe with what we do, even when no one is watching. This internal alignment manifests as honesty, courage, empathy, and responsibility, qualities that resonate with authenticity and moral strength. A person of strong character does not merely profess their values but embodies them in every aspect of their life, from grand decisions to everyday interactions.

Character is what defines our moral fiber. It is an amalgamation of our beliefs, our attitudes, and our behaviors, all intricately woven together to create the essence of who we are. It is not something that can be put on or taken off depending on circumstances; rather, it is an intrinsic part of our identity. Our character is revealed in our actions and decisions, especially in moments of adversity when our true values are tested.

Integrity: The Cornerstone of Character

One of the most defining aspects of character is integrity. Integrity is the unwavering adherence to moral and ethical principles, regardless of the circumstances. It involves doing what is right, even when it is difficult or inconvenient. Integrity builds trust and respect, laying a foundation for genuine relationships and meaningful connections. It is the quality that ensures our actions are congruent with our values, fostering a sense of reliability and consistency.

Integrity is more than just honesty; it is the alignment of our thoughts, words, and actions. It requires us to be truthful not only with others but also with ourselves. When we live with integrity, we are consistent in our ethical standards, and this consistency earns us the trust and respect of those around us. Integrity means standing by our principles even when it is challenging, and not compromising our values for short-term gains.

In professional settings, integrity is crucial for building strong, trustworthy relationships with colleagues, clients, and stakeholders. Leaders who demonstrate integrity create a culture of honesty and transparency within their organizations, which in turn fosters loyalty and commitment among employees. This culture of integrity extends beyond the workplace, influencing how businesses interact with society at large, and shaping their reputation and legacy.

Resilience: The Strength of Character

Another critical component of character is resilience. Life is replete with challenges, setbacks, and adversities, and resilience is the capacity to endure and overcome these obstacles with grace and perseverance. Resilient individuals face difficulties with a positive outlook, learning from their experiences and emerging stronger. This strength of character enables us to navigate life's storms, adapt to change, and maintain hope even in the face of adversity.

Resilience is not about avoiding difficulties but rather about facing them head-on and finding ways to overcome them. It involves the ability to recover from setbacks, to maintain a positive attitude, and to continue moving forward even when the going gets tough. Resilient individuals are able to bounce back from failures and disappointments, using these experiences as opportunities for growth and learning.

The resilience of character is particularly important in times of crisis or uncertainty. Whether dealing with personal challenges, such as illness or loss, or navigating larger societal upheavals, resilience helps us to stay grounded and focused. It allows us to maintain our sense of purpose and direction, even when circumstances are difficult, and to emerge from adversity with a renewed sense of strength and determination.

Empathy: The Heart of Character

Empathy is also a cornerstone of character. It involves the ability to understand and share the feelings of others, to walk in their shoes, and to respond with compassion. Empathetic individuals connect with others on a deep emotional level, fostering trust and mutual respect. This quality is essential for building strong relationships, resolving conflicts, and creating a supportive and inclusive environment. Empathy enriches our interactions and enhances our capacity to contribute positively to the lives of those around us.

Empathy is not just about feeling sympathy for others; it is about actively engaging with their emotions and experiences. It requires us to listen deeply, to be present with others in their moments of joy and sorrow, and to offer support without judgment. Empathy allows us to connect with others in a meaningful way, creating bonds of trust and understanding that are the foundation of healthy relationships.

In leadership and professional contexts, empathy is essential for creating a positive and inclusive work environment. Leaders who demonstrate empathy are able to connect with their team members on a personal level, understanding their needs, concerns, and motivations. This understanding allows leaders to create a supportive environment where individuals feel valued and appreciated, and where they are motivated to perform at their best.

Responsibility: The Obligation of Character

Responsibility is another key element of character. It is the acknowledgment and acceptance of our duties and obligations, both to ourselves and to others. Responsible individuals take ownership of their actions, make informed decisions, and are accountable for their consequences. This sense of responsibility ensures that we contribute meaningfully to our communities, uphold our commitments, and strive to make a positive impact on the world.

Being responsible means recognizing the impact of our actions on others and the world around us. It involves making choices that are aligned with our values and being accountable for the outcomes of those choices. Responsible individuals do not shy away from difficult decisions or from the consequences of their actions; instead, they face them with integrity and courage.

Responsibility also extends to our role in society and the environment. As members of a global community, we have a responsibility to contribute to the greater good, to act in ways that promote justice, equality, and sustainability. This responsibility requires us to be informed, to be engaged, and to take action in ways that reflect our values and principles.

The Dynamic Nature of Character

Character is not a static trait but a dynamic and evolving aspect of our lives. It is shaped by our experiences, choices, and reflections, and it requires continual growth and self-awareness. Developing strong character involves ongoing self-examination, a willingness to learn from mistakes, and a commitment to personal growth. It is a lifelong journey of striving to align our actions with our values, to build on our strengths, and to address our weaknesses.

The development of character is an ongoing process that requires continuous effort and reflection. It involves examining our values and beliefs, and making choices that are aligned with those values. It also involves recognizing and addressing our weaknesses, and striving to improve ourselves in ways that reflect our commitment to integrity, resilience, empathy, and responsibility.

The dynamic nature of character means that it is not something that can be taken for granted; it must be nurtured and developed over time. This requires a commitment to personal growth and self-improvement, and a willingness to confront our limitations and challenges. By continuously striving to develop our character, we can build a foundation of integrity, resilience, empathy, and responsibility that will guide us throughout our lives.

The Influence of Character in Society

The influence of character extends beyond individual interactions and personal development; it shapes our broader social and cultural environments. Leaders, educators, and influencers who exemplify strong character inspire others, set standards, and drive positive change. Their integrity, empathy, and responsibility create a ripple effect, impacting their communities and fostering a culture of trust and respect.

Character is not only a personal trait but also a social force that can influence others and shape society. Leaders who demonstrate strong character are able to inspire and motivate others to act with integrity and responsibility. They set a standard for ethical behavior and create a culture of trust and respect within their organizations and communities.

Educators also play a crucial role in shaping the character of future generations. By modeling integrity, empathy, and responsibility, educators can instill these values in their students and help them develop the character traits that will guide them throughout their lives. This influence extends beyond the classroom, as students carry these values with them into their families, communities, and workplaces.

In the broader social context, individuals who exemplify strong character can have a powerful impact on society as a whole. They can influence public opinion, shape social norms, and drive positive change by advocating for justice, equality, and sustainability. By demonstrating integrity, resilience, empathy, and responsibility, these individuals can inspire others to do the same, creating a ripple effect that can lead to a more just and compassionate world.

Character in an Interconnected World

In our increasingly interconnected world, character continues to serve as a pillar of authenticity and moral clarity. Amidst the noise of superficiality and the pursuit of material success, character stands as a reminder of what truly matters. It is the foundation upon which we build our legacies, the measure of our true impact, and the essence of our humanity.

In a world that is often driven by external validation and material success, character serves as a grounding force that reminds us of our core values and principles. It is a constant in a world that is constantly changing, providing us with a sense of stability and direction. By staying true to our character, we can navigate the complexities of life with integrity and purpose, and create a legacy that reflects our true worth.

Character is also essential for building trust and credibility in an interconnected world. In a globalized society, where interactions and relationships often transcend borders and cultures, character serves as a universal language of trust and respect. Individuals and organizations that demonstrate strong character are able to build lasting relationships and create a positive impact on the world.

As we navigate the challenges and opportunities of an interconnected world, character will continue to be a guiding force that shapes our actions and decisions. By staying true to our values and principles, and by demonstrating integrity, resilience, empathy, and responsibility, we can build a world that reflects the best of our humanity.

CHAPTER 22
VALUE

"Try not to become a man of success, but rather try to become a man of value." — Albert Einstein

Value: The Core of Human Experience and Decision-Making

Value is a concept that permeates every aspect of human life, influencing our decisions, relationships, and the way we perceive the world around us. At its core, value represents the importance or worth we assign to something, whether it be a material object, a principle, or an experience. Understanding what we value and why we value it is crucial in shaping our identities and guiding our actions.

The Subjectivity of Value

The notion of value is inherently subjective, varying greatly from person to person and culture to culture. What one individual might hold as invaluable, another may consider trivial. This subjectivity is often influenced by personal experiences, cultural background, education, and societal norms. For example, in some cultures, family and community might be the highest values, while in others, individual achievement and success might take precedence. The diversity in what people value is a reflection of the rich tapestry of human experience and thought.

The subjectivity of value also means that our personal values can be deeply tied to our identities. They reflect our unique life experiences, our aspirations, and our understanding of what is meaningful. This subjectivity can sometimes lead to conflicts when values clash, but it also allows for a rich diversity of perspectives and ways of life. Understanding and respecting this subjectivity is key to navigating relationships and interactions in a multicultural and pluralistic society.

Tangible vs. Intangible Values

Value can be understood in both tangible and intangible terms. Tangible values are those that can be measured or quantified, such as the monetary value of an object or the utility it provides. For instance, the value of money is clear in its ability to purchase goods and services. However, even within this realm, value is not absolute. The same amount of money may hold different significance for different people based on their financial situation, needs, and goals.

Intangible values, on the other hand, are those that are less easily measured but often hold profound significance in our lives. These include values like love, integrity, honesty, and compassion. These are the principles that guide our moral compass, the standards by which we judge our actions and the actions of others. Intangible values are often what we turn to when making difficult decisions, serving as a framework for determining what is right or wrong, good or bad.

The interplay between tangible and intangible values is evident in many aspects of life. For example, the decision to pursue a career in a high-paying field versus one that offers personal fulfillment reflects a balance (or conflict) between tangible and intangible values. Similarly, the choice to spend money on material goods versus donating to charity highlights the contrast between valuing material wealth and valuing altruism or community well-being.

Values in Decision-Making

One of the most significant aspects of value is its role in decision-making. Every decision we make, whether large or small, is influenced by what we value. From choosing a career path to deciding how to spend our free time, our choices reflect our underlying values. For example, someone who values financial security may prioritize a stable job with a steady income, while someone who values adventure and new experiences may opt for a career that allows for travel and exploration. In this way, our values act as a compass, guiding us toward decisions that align with what we find meaningful and important.

Decision-making based on values is not always a straightforward process. It often involves weighing competing values and making trade-offs. For instance, a person might have to choose between spending time with family (valuing relationships) and working extra hours to achieve a promotion (valuing career success). These decisions require careful reflection and a clear understanding of one's priorities.

Moreover, the values that guide our decisions are not always consciously recognized. Sometimes, it is only after we reflect on a decision that we realize which values were at play. This is why self-awareness and introspection are crucial for aligning our decisions with our true values. By regularly examining our choices and the values behind them, we can ensure that our actions are consistent with our principles and that we are living in a way that is authentic to who we are.

Values in Relationships

In relationships, value plays a crucial role in determining how we connect with others. We are naturally drawn to people who share similar values because these shared values create a sense of understanding and common ground. This is why values are often at the heart of strong friendships, partnerships, and communities. When we value honesty, we seek out relationships built on trust and transparency. When we value kindness, we are more likely to form connections with those who are compassionate and empathetic. Conversely, when values clash, it can lead to conflict and misunderstanding. For example, a relationship where one person values independence while the other values closeness and interdependence might struggle without mutual respect and compromise.

Values are important not only in personal relationships but also in professional and social interactions. In the workplace, shared values can create a strong organizational culture where employees feel aligned with the company's mission and goals. In social groups, common values can foster a sense of belonging and community. However, when values are not shared or respected, it can lead to tension and division.

Navigating relationships where values differ requires open communication, empathy, and a willingness to understand and respect the other person's perspective. It also requires setting boundaries and finding compromises that allow both parties to feel valued and respected. In some cases, it may be necessary to reassess the relationship and determine whether it is possible to reconcile the differing values or whether it is best to part ways.

Values and Identity

Values are also integral to our sense of identity. The things we hold dear, the principles we live by, and the priorities we set for ourselves all contribute to our self-concept. When we live in accordance with our values, we experience a sense of authenticity and fulfillment. This alignment between our actions and our values is often referred to as "living with integrity." Conversely, when our actions contradict our values, we may experience inner conflict, guilt, or dissatisfaction.

Living in alignment with our values is crucial for our mental and emotional well-being. It allows us to live authentically and to feel a sense of purpose and direction in our lives. When our actions are congruent with our values, we experience a sense of harmony and balance. This integrity is not only important for our own well-being but also for building trust and credibility in our relationships with others.

However, living in alignment with our values is not always easy. It requires self-awareness, courage, and a willingness to stand by our principles even when it is difficult or unpopular. It may involve making difficult decisions or facing criticism from others. But by staying true to our values, we can build a life that is meaningful and fulfilling, and we can inspire others to do the same.

The Evolution of Values

The process of identifying and understanding our values is an ongoing journey. It requires self-reflection, introspection, and sometimes, challenging life experiences. Often, our values become clearer during times of crisis or when faced with difficult decisions. For instance, someone who has always valued career success may, after a personal loss, realize that family and relationships hold greater importance. This shift in values can lead to a re-evaluation of life choices and priorities.

Moreover, our values can evolve over time as we grow, learn, and encounter new experiences. What we value in our youth may differ significantly from what we value as we age. This evolution of values is a natural part of personal development and is often influenced by the changing circumstances of our lives. As we navigate different stages of life, we may find that certain values take precedence over others, reflecting our current needs, goals, and understanding of the world.

The evolution of values is also influenced by the broader cultural and social context in which we live. As society changes, our values may shift in response to new ideas, technologies, and social movements. For example, the growing awareness of environmental issues has led many people to place greater value on sustainability and conservation. Similarly, the increasing focus on mental health and well-being has led to a greater emphasis on self-care and work-life balance.

Values in Societal Context

In the broader societal context, values shape cultures, laws, and social norms. Societies are built on shared values, which form the foundation for social cohesion and collective identity. These shared values are often reflected in a society's laws, traditions, and institutions. For example, a society that values freedom and equality will strive to create systems that promote individual rights and social justice. On a global scale, the clash or convergence of different cultural values can lead to conflict or cooperation, shaping international relations and global dynamics.

Values are important not only for individuals but also for communities and societies as a whole. Shared values create a sense of unity and common purpose, helping to build strong and resilient communities. They provide a framework for resolving conflicts, making collective decisions, and addressing social challenges. However, when values are not shared or when they come into conflict, it can lead to division and polarization.

In a multicultural and interconnected world, understanding and respecting different values is crucial for building peaceful and inclusive societies. This requires open dialogue, empathy, and a willingness to find common ground. It also requires a commitment to justice and equality, ensuring that all individuals and groups are treated with respect and dignity, regardless of their values or beliefs.

The Role of Values in Shaping Behavior

Ultimately, value is about what we hold as important and worthy of our time, energy, and resources. It is a reflection of our priorities, guiding our actions and shaping our lives. Whether tangible or intangible, personal or societal, values are the driving force behind human behavior and interaction, by understanding and honoring our values, we can live more purposeful and fulfilling lives, making decisions that resonate with our true selves.

Values influence our behavior in both conscious and unconscious ways. They shape our attitudes, beliefs, and actions, guiding us in our interactions with others and in the choices we make. For example, someone who values honesty will strive to be truthful in their interactions, while someone who values compassion will seek to help others and alleviate suffering.

Understanding our values is crucial for making intentional and deliberate choices. When we are clear about what we value, we can make decisions that are aligned with our principles and that reflect our true priorities. This intentionality allows us to live with greater purpose and fulfillment, and to build a life that is meaningful and satisfying.

The Intersection of Values and Ethics

Values are closely related to ethics, as they form the foundation for our moral judgments and decisions. Ethics is the study of what is right and wrong, and values are the principles that guide our understanding of these concepts. Our values inform our ethical beliefs, shaping our understanding of what is good and just, and influencing our behavior and decisions.

The intersection of values and ethics is evident in many aspects of life, from personal relationships to professional conduct to social and political issues. For example, ethical decisions in the workplace are often guided by values such as honesty, integrity, and fairness. Similarly, social and political movements are often driven by values such as justice, equality, and human rights.

Understanding the relationship between values and ethics is crucial for making ethical decisions and for navigating complex moral dilemmas. It requires self-awareness, critical thinking, and a commitment to acting in ways that reflect our principles and that promote the greater good.

The Impact of Values on Well-Being

Values also have a significant impact on our well-being. When we live in alignment with our values, we experience a sense of authenticity and fulfillment. This alignment allows us to live with integrity and to build a life that is meaningful and satisfying.

Conversely, when our actions are not aligned with our values, we may experience inner conflict, guilt, or dissatisfaction.

Living in alignment with our values is crucial for our mental and emotional well-being. It allows us to live authentically and to feel a sense of purpose and direction in our lives. When our actions are congruent with our values, we experience a sense of harmony and balance. This integrity is not only important for our own well-being but also for building trust and credibility in our relationships with others.

Moreover, values are closely linked to our sense of identity and self-worth. When we live in accordance with our values, we feel a sense of pride and satisfaction in who we are. This self-esteem is crucial for our overall well-being and for building positive and healthy relationships with others.

The Enduring Significance of Values

Values are subjective, varying from person to person and culture to culture. They can be tangible or intangible, personal or societal. Values play a crucial role in decision-making, relationships, identity, and well-being. They influence our behavior, shape our ethical beliefs, and guide us in making intentional and deliberate choices.

The process of identifying and understanding our values is an ongoing journey that requires self-reflection, introspection, and sometimes, challenging life experiences. Our values can evolve over time as we grow, learn, and encounter new experiences. In the broader societal context, values shape cultures, laws, and social norms, and they are crucial for building strong and resilient communities.

By understanding and honoring our values, we can live more purposeful and fulfilling lives, making decisions that resonate with our true selves. Values are the driving force behind human behavior and interaction, and they are the foundation for building a life that is meaningful, satisfying, and authentic.

CHAPTER 23
HARMONY

"He who lives in harmony with himself lives in harmony with the universe." — Marcus Aurelius

Harmony: The Art of Balance and Unity in Life

In its simplest form, harmony can be understood as the smooth interaction of various components within a system. Whether in nature, music, relationships, or society, harmony exists when there is a balanced arrangement of diverse elements, each contributing to the whole while maintaining its unique identity. For instance, in music, harmony arises when different notes are played together to produce a pleasing sound. Each note retains its distinct pitch, yet when combined, they create chords that enrich the musical piece. Similarly, in nature, harmony is observed in ecosystems where different species coexist and interact in a balanced way, supporting each other's survival and contributing to the overall health of the environment.

Harmony is a concept that resonates deeply within the human experience, embodying the balance, unity, and interconnectedness that we often seek in our lives. It represents a state of peaceful coexistence, where different elements—whether they be individuals, ideas, or actions—blend together seamlessly to create something greater than the sum of their parts. Harmony is not merely the absence of conflict; it is the presence of an intentional and thoughtful alignment that nurtures growth, understanding, and mutual respect.

Harmony in Human Relationships

Harmony in human relationships is essential for fostering a sense of connection and belonging. It is about finding common ground, respecting differences, and working together toward shared goals. In a harmonious relationship, there is mutual understanding and appreciation of each other's perspectives, needs, and values. This does not mean that disagreements or conflicts do not exist; rather, it means that when they arise, they are addressed with empathy, open communication, and a willingness to compromise. Harmony is achieved when all parties feel heard, valued, and understood, leading to stronger, more resilient connections.

Relationships, whether they are between family members, friends, or colleagues, thrive on harmony. It creates an environment where trust and respect can flourish and where individuals can express themselves freely without fear of judgment or rejection. In families, for example, harmony fosters unity and a sense of safety, where members support one another and work together to overcome challenges. In friendships, harmony is the glue that holds people together, allowing for meaningful and lasting connections. In the workplace, harmonious relationships among colleagues lead to better teamwork, increased productivity, and a more positive work environment.

Harmony in Society

In a broader societal context, harmony is crucial for creating cohesive communities and promoting social stability. A harmonious society is one where diversity is celebrated and different cultural, religious, and social groups coexist peacefully. This requires a commitment to justice, equality, and respect for human rights. It also involves actively working to resolve conflicts, reduce inequalities, and promote inclusivity. When harmony prevails in society, individuals are more likely to cooperate, trust one another, and contribute positively to the community. This collective sense of harmony can lead to a more just and equitable world where everyone has the opportunity to thrive.

Societal harmony is built on the foundations of shared values, mutual respect, and a commitment to the common good. It is achieved when individuals and groups recognize their interdependence and work together to create a society that benefits all its members. This involves addressing social injustices, bridging cultural divides, and fostering dialogue and understanding across different communities. In a harmonious society, differences are not seen as threats but as opportunities for learning and growth.

Inner Harmony

The pursuit of harmony is also central to personal well-being. Inner harmony, or the alignment of one's thoughts, emotions, and actions, is a key component of mental and emotional health. When we are in harmony with ourselves, we experience a sense of peace, clarity, and purpose. This inner balance allows us to navigate life's challenges with greater resilience and to make decisions that are in line with our true values and desires. Achieving inner harmony often requires self-reflection, mindfulness, and a commitment to personal growth. It involves recognizing and addressing internal conflicts, managing stress, and fostering a positive relationship with oneself.

Inner harmony is about finding a balance between our aspirations and our reality, between our needs and our responsibilities, and between our personal desires and the demands of the world around us. It is about living authentically, in alignment with our true selves, and finding peace in who we are. This requires regular introspection, a willingness to confront our fears and insecurities, and a commitment to living according to our values.

Harmony with Nature

Harmony with nature is another important aspect of living a balanced and fulfilling life. Our relationship with the natural world has a profound impact on our well-being, as well as on the health of the planet. Living in harmony with nature means recognizing our interdependence with the environment and making choices that support sustainability and ecological balance. This can involve adopting practices that reduce our environmental footprint, such as conserving energy, reducing waste, and supporting sustainable agriculture. It also means advocating for policies and initiatives that protect natural ecosystems and biodiversity. By living in harmony with nature, we contribute to the preservation of the planet for future generations and enhance our own sense of connection to the world around us.

Harmony with nature also involves cultivating a sense of reverence and respect for the natural world. It means recognizing that we are not separate from nature but a part of it and that our well-being is intimately connected to the health of the environment. This awareness can lead to a more mindful and responsible way of living, where we make choices that are in harmony with the earth's natural rhythms and cycles.

The Challenges of Achieving Harmony

Harmony is not always easy to achieve, especially in a world marked by complexity, diversity, and competing interests. It requires ongoing effort, patience, and a willingness to embrace differences rather than resist them. It also involves a commitment to continuous learning and adaptation, as the conditions for harmony can change over time. For example, as societies become more diverse, new challenges may arise in maintaining social harmony, requiring innovative approaches to conflict resolution, education, and community building.

In personal relationships, achieving harmony often requires compromise, understanding, and a willingness to put the needs of others before our own. It involves listening deeply, communicating openly, and being willing to let go of our ego and pride. In society, achieving harmony requires a commitment to justice and equality, as well as a willingness to address and resolve conflicts in a peaceful and constructive manner.

Harmony in the Workplace

In the workplace, harmony is essential for fostering a positive and productive environment. When team members work harmoniously, there is greater collaboration, creativity, and efficiency. This is because harmony in the workplace reduces stress, increases job satisfaction, and enhances communication. To cultivate harmony in professional settings, it is important to promote inclusivity, encourage open dialogue, and recognize and celebrate the unique contributions of each team member. Leadership plays a crucial role in setting the tone for harmony, as leaders who prioritize fairness, transparency, and respect create a culture where harmony can thrive.

Workplace harmony is not just about creating a pleasant environment; it is also about creating a culture where everyone feels valued and respected, where diversity is embraced, and where collaboration and teamwork are encouraged. This requires leaders who are skilled in conflict resolution, who are able to create a vision that unites the team, and who are committed to fostering a culture of trust and mutual respect.

The Role of Harmony in Personal Growth

Harmony also plays a crucial role in personal growth and development. When we are in harmony with ourselves and with others, we are more likely to experience a sense of fulfillment and satisfaction in our lives. This inner harmony allows us to pursue our goals with clarity and focus, to build meaningful relationships, and to live with a sense of purpose and direction.

Personal growth often involves finding harmony between different aspects of our lives, such as our work and personal life, our needs and the needs of others, and our desires and responsibilities. It requires a commitment to continuous learning and self-improvement, as well as a willingness to confront and resolve internal and external conflicts.

The Spiritual Dimension of Harmony

Harmony also has a spiritual dimension. Many spiritual traditions emphasize the importance of harmony, both within ourselves and in our relationships with others and with the natural world. In these traditions, harmony is seen as a reflection of the divine order, a state of balance and unity that reflects the underlying harmony of the universe.

In this context, achieving harmony is not just about creating peace and balance in our lives; it is also about aligning ourselves with the greater harmony of the cosmos. This requires a deep sense of reverence and respect for the interconnectedness of all things, as well as a commitment to living in a way that is in harmony with the natural and spiritual laws of the universe.

The Importance of Harmony in Global Relations

In the context of global relations, harmony is crucial for promoting peace and cooperation between nations. In an increasingly interconnected world, where conflicts and tensions can have far-reaching consequences, finding ways to build harmony between different cultures, religions, and political systems is more important than ever.

This requires a commitment to dialogue and understanding, as well as a willingness to find common ground and work towards shared goals. It also requires a recognition of our shared humanity and a commitment to justice, equality, and human rights. By promoting harmony in global relations, we can create a world that is more peaceful, just, and sustainable.

The Benefits of Living in Harmony

Living in harmony, whether within ourselves, with others, or with the natural world, has numerous benefits. It leads to greater peace and contentment, improved relationships, and a deeper sense of connection and purpose. It also enhances our ability to cope with life's challenges, reduces stress and anxiety, and promotes overall well-being.

In addition, living in harmony contributes to the well-being of others and to the health and sustainability of our planet. By making choices that are in harmony with our values, with the needs of others, and with the natural world, we can create a life that is not only fulfilling and meaningful but also contributes to the greater good.

The Enduring Value of Harmony

Harmony is a concept that touches every aspect of our lives. It is about finding balance, fostering unity, and creating conditions where different elements can coexist peacefully and productively. Whether in our personal relationships, communities, workplaces, or in our relationship with nature, harmony is essential for well-being, growth, and sustainability. While achieving harmony may require effort and intentionality, the rewards are profound. A life lived in harmony is one marked by peace, fulfillment, and a deep sense of connection to oneself and others.

Harmony is not just a state of being; it is a way of living, a way of interacting with the world that reflects our deepest values and our highest aspirations. It is about creating a world where diversity is celebrated, where conflicts are resolved peacefully, and where everyone has the opportunity to thrive. It is about living in a way that is true to ourselves, that honors the needs and rights of others, and that is in harmony with the natural world.

By embracing harmony in all aspects of our lives, we can create a world that is more just, more peaceful, and more sustainable. We can create a life that is more fulfilling, more meaningful, and more connected. And in doing so, we can contribute to the greater harmony of the world, helping to create a future that is bright with hope, possibility, and peace.

CHAPTER 24
KNOWLEDGE

"Learning never exhausts the mind." — Leonardo da Vinci

Knowledge: The Pillar of Human Progress and Personal Growth

Knowledge, the vast expanse of human understanding and insight, forms the foundation of our civilization and personal growth. It is the driving force behind progress, innovation, and our ability to comprehend the world around us. Knowledge encompasses facts, information, skills, and wisdom accumulated through experience, education, and intellectual exploration. It is both the accumulation of data and the ability to apply that data in meaningful ways, influencing every aspect of our lives and shaping the trajectory of society.

The Foundations of Knowledge

At its core, knowledge is the foundation of learning and development. From the moment we are born, we begin to gather knowledge through sensory experiences, observation, and interaction with our environment. As we grow, formal education introduces us to structured forms of knowledge, ranging from basic literacy and numeracy to complex scientific theories and philosophical concepts. This education is not just about memorizing facts but about developing critical thinking skills that enable us to analyze, interpret, and apply information effectively.

The pursuit of knowledge is a fundamental human drive. It motivates us to explore the unknown, question established norms, and seek out new understanding. Throughout history, the quest for knowledge has led to groundbreaking discoveries and advancements that have transformed societies. The scientific revolution, for example, was driven by a desire to understand the natural world, leading to profound changes in technology, medicine, and our understanding of the universe. Similarly, advancements in fields like psychology, sociology, and economics have expanded our understanding of human behavior and societal dynamics, leading to improved quality of life and social progress.

The Evolution of Knowledge

Knowledge is not static but continually evolving. Each generation builds upon the knowledge of the previous one, refining theories, correcting misconceptions, and expanding our understanding. This dynamic nature of knowledge is reflected in the scientific method, which relies on observation, experimentation, and revision to advance our comprehension of the natural world. As new discoveries are made and technologies advance, our collective knowledge base grows, leading to new questions and further exploration.

The value of knowledge extends beyond the academic and scientific realms; it also influences our personal lives and relationships. Knowledge about ourselves, our values, and our goals guide our decisions and actions. It helps us navigate complex situations, understand different perspectives, and develop empathy for others. Emotional intelligence, for instance, is a form of knowledge that allows us to recognize and manage our emotions and those of others, fostering healthier relationships and effective communication.

The Digital Age and the Accessibility of Knowledge

In the digital age, the accessibility of knowledge has increased exponentially. The internet, with its vast repositories of information, has transformed how we acquire and share knowledge. Online resources, educational platforms, and digital libraries provide unprecedented access to information, enabling individuals to learn and grow in ways that were once unimaginable. However, this abundance of information also presents challenges, such as discerning credible sources from misinformation and navigating the sheer volume of available data. Critical thinking and media literacy have become essential skills in effectively managing and utilizing the wealth of information at our fingertips.

The digital era has also democratized knowledge, making it accessible to people across the globe, irrespective of geographical boundaries or economic status. Free online courses, open-access journals, and virtual classrooms have opened doors to learning for millions. However, this easy access also comes with the responsibility to critically assess the quality of information, as the internet can be a source of both accurate knowledge and widespread misinformation.

Knowledge and Global Challenges

Knowledge plays a crucial role in addressing global challenges. Issues such as climate change, public health, and social inequality require informed solutions and collaborative efforts. Scientific research, policy analysis, and interdisciplinary approaches contribute to our understanding of these complex problems and inform strategies for addressing them. The application of knowledge in these areas not only helps us solve immediate challenges but also lays the groundwork for sustainable development and future progress.

For instance, the global response to the COVID-19 pandemic highlighted the importance of scientific knowledge and international collaboration. Scientists around the world worked tirelessly to understand the virus, develop vaccines, and implement public health measures. This collective effort underscored how crucial knowledge is in responding to crises and protecting public health.

Moreover, the ethical dimensions of knowledge are increasingly important. As we advance our understanding and capabilities, we must consider the ethical implications of our actions and decisions.

The use of technology, such as artificial intelligence and genetic engineering, raises questions about privacy, consent, and the potential for unintended consequences. Ethical considerations guide us in applying knowledge responsibly and ensuring that advancements benefit humanity as a whole.

Knowledge, Creativity, and Innovation

The pursuit of knowledge is also deeply connected to creativity and innovation. The ability to think critically and imaginatively enables us to solve problems in novel ways and develop new solutions. Many of the greatest innovations in history have arisen from the intersection of knowledge and creativity, where understanding is applied in imaginative and groundbreaking ways. For example, the development of the internet, a transformative innovation, emerged from a combination of technological knowledge and creative thinking.

Creativity, fueled by knowledge, leads to innovation across all fields, from technology and medicine to the arts and social sciences. The invention of the airplane, the discovery of DNA's structure, and the creation of the World Wide Web all exemplify how knowledge, when combined with creativity, can lead to transformative advancements. These innovations have not only solved problems but have also opened up new possibilities for exploration and development.

Knowledge and Personal Fulfillment

In addition to its practical applications, knowledge enriches our lives in profound ways. It inspires curiosity, fosters a sense of wonder, and connects us to a larger human experience. Literature, art, and philosophy, as forms of knowledge, provide insight into the human condition, explore existential questions, and offer reflections on our place in the world. Engaging with these forms of knowledge can lead to personal growth, emotional enrichment, and a deeper appreciation for the diversity of human experience.

The arts and humanities, often undervalued in comparison to scientific knowledge, play a critical role in our understanding of the world and ourselves. Through literature, we explore different cultures, histories, and perspectives, gaining empathy and insight. Through art, we express emotions, confront social issues, and celebrate beauty. Philosophy challenges us to question our beliefs, consider ethical dilemmas, and seek meaning in our existence. These forms of knowledge contribute to a richer, more nuanced understanding of the world and our place in it.

The Collective and Personal Value of Knowledge

Ultimately, knowledge is both a personal and collective asset. On an individual level, it empowers us to make informed choices, pursue our passions, and contribute meaningfully to our communities. On a collective level, it drives societal progress, fosters collaboration, and addresses global challenges. The continuous pursuit and application of knowledge are essential for personal fulfillment and societal advancement.

Knowledge is the foundation upon which civilizations are built and sustained. It is through the accumulation, preservation, and dissemination of knowledge that societies advance, cultures thrive, and individuals find their place in the world. Libraries, universities, research institutions, and educational systems are the custodians of knowledge, ensuring that it is passed down from generation to generation.

The value of knowledge extends beyond practical utility; it is also intrinsically valuable. The pursuit of knowledge satisfies our innate curiosity, our desire to understand the world and our place in it. It connects us to the past, helps us navigate the present, and prepares us for the future. It enriches our lives, providing us with the tools to think critically, solve problems, and make informed decisions.

The Role of Knowledge in Empowering Individuals

On a personal level, knowledge empowers individuals by providing them with the tools they need to navigate the world. It allows us to make informed decisions, solve problems, and achieve our goals. Knowledge also fosters a sense of self-confidence and autonomy, as it equips us with the information and skills necessary to take control of our lives.

Education, in particular, plays a crucial role in empowering individuals. By providing access to knowledge, education opens up opportunities for personal and professional growth. It enables individuals to pursue their passions, develop their talents, and contribute meaningfully to society. Education also promotes social mobility, allowing individuals to improve their circumstances and achieve their aspirations.

In the workplace, knowledge is a key factor in determining success and advancement. Employees with specialized knowledge and skills are often more competitive in the job market and more likely to achieve their career goals. Continuous learning and professional development are essential for staying relevant in an ever-changing job market. As industries evolve and new technologies emerge, the ability to acquire and apply new knowledge becomes increasingly important.

The Role of Knowledge in Social and Economic Development

On a broader scale, knowledge plays a vital role in social and economic development. Societies that prioritize education and invest in research and innovation are more likely to experience economic growth, social progress, and improved quality of life. Knowledge-based economies, where the production and use of knowledge are key drivers of economic activity, have become increasingly important in the global landscape.

The importance of knowledge in economic development is evident in the success of countries that have prioritized education, research, and innovation. For example, countries like South Korea and Singapore have transformed their economies by investing in education, technology, and infrastructure, becoming leaders in various industries. These knowledge-based economies are characterized by high levels of education, technological innovation, and a strong emphasis on research and development.

In addition to economic benefits, knowledge also plays a crucial role in social development. Access to education and information empowers individuals to participate fully in society, exercise their rights, and contribute to the democratic process. Knowledge also promotes social cohesion by fostering understanding and tolerance among diverse groups. It enables individuals to engage with complex social issues, challenge injustice, and advocate for change.

The Ethical Dimensions of Knowledge

As we continue to advance our understanding and capabilities, the ethical dimensions of knowledge become increasingly important. The use of knowledge, particularly in fields like technology, medicine, and the environment, raises ethical questions that must be carefully considered. Issues such as privacy, consent, and the potential for unintended consequences require us to think critically about how we apply knowledge and the impact it may have on individuals and society.

In the field of technology, for example, the development and use of artificial intelligence raise ethical concerns about privacy, security, and the potential for bias and discrimination. The ability of AI systems to analyze vast amounts of data and make decisions based on that data has the potential to revolutionize industries, but it also poses significant risks if not managed responsibly.

In medicine, advancements in genetic engineering and biotechnology raise ethical questions about the manipulation of human genes, the potential for unintended consequences, and the implications for future generations. The ability to edit the human genome has the potential to cure genetic diseases, but it also raises concerns about the ethics of altering human DNA and the potential for unintended consequences.

Environmental ethics also plays a crucial role in our understanding of the impact of human activities on the natural world. As we continue to advance our knowledge of environmental issues, we must consider the ethical implications of our actions and make decisions that prioritize sustainability and the preservation of the planet.

The Role of Knowledge in Fostering Global Collaboration

In a world that is increasingly interconnected, knowledge plays a crucial role in fostering global collaboration and addressing shared challenges. Issues such as climate change, public health, and social inequality require informed solutions and collaborative efforts that transcend national borders. The sharing of knowledge, research, and expertise across countries and disciplines is essential for finding effective solutions to these complex problems.

International organizations, such as the United Nations, the World Health Organization, and the World Bank, play a crucial role in facilitating the sharing of knowledge and expertise across countries. These organizations bring together experts from different fields and countries to collaborate on solutions to global challenges. They also provide a platform for sharing best practices, lessons learned, and innovative approaches to addressing shared challenges.

The Future of Knowledge

As we look to the future, the pursuit and application of knowledge will continue to play a crucial role in shaping our world. The rapid pace of technological advancement, the increasing complexity of global challenges, and the growing importance of sustainability will require us to think critically and creatively about how we acquire and apply knowledge.

The digital age has transformed how we access and share knowledge, and this trend is likely to continue in the future. Advances in artificial intelligence, big data, and machine learning have the potential to revolutionize how we acquire, process, and apply knowledge. These technologies will enable us to analyze vast amounts of data, identify patterns, and make predictions with greater accuracy and speed than ever before.

However, as we continue to advance our knowledge and capabilities, we must also consider the ethical implications of our actions and decisions. The use of technology, particularly in fields like artificial intelligence and genetic engineering, raises ethical questions that must be carefully considered. We must ensure that the advancements we make are used responsibly and that they benefit humanity as a whole.

The Power and Responsibility of Knowledge

In conclusion, knowledge is a force that shapes our understanding of the world and ourselves. It drives progress, fosters personal growth, and influences every aspect of our lives. As we continue to explore, learn, and apply our knowledge, we contribute to the ongoing evolution of human understanding and the betterment of society. Embracing the pursuit of knowledge with curiosity, critical thinking, and ethical considerations ensures that we harness its potential to create a more informed, compassionate, and innovative world.

Knowledge is not just about acquiring information; it is about understanding, applying, and sharing that information in ways that benefit individuals and society. It is about questioning assumptions, challenging the status quo, and seeking out new understanding. It is about using our knowledge to make informed decisions, solve problems, and contribute meaningfully to the world.

As we continue to advance our knowledge and capabilities, we must also consider the ethical implications of our actions and decisions. We must ensure that the advancements we make are used responsibly and that they benefit humanity as a whole. The pursuit of knowledge is a lifelong journey, and it is up to each of us to embrace it with curiosity, integrity, and a commitment to making the world a better place for future generations.

CHAPTER 25
RESPONSIBILITY

"We are made wise not by the recollection of our past, but by the responsibility for our future." – George Bernard Shaw

Responsibility: The Cornerstone of Human Experience and Interaction

Responsibility is a fundamental principle that shapes every aspect of human experience and interaction. It is a concept that encapsulates our duty to act with accountability, integrity, and ethical consideration. At its core, responsibility involves the ability to make decisions, fulfill obligations, and take ownership of our actions and their consequences. It is a quality that influences how we navigate our personal lives, interact with others, and contribute to society.

Responsibility in Personal Life

In personal life, responsibility manifests as the ability to manage our own affairs effectively. This includes setting and achieving goals, managing time and resources wisely, and maintaining self-discipline. Personal responsibility is about making choices that reflect our values and understanding how these choices impact our own lives and those around us. It requires self-awareness and the willingness to reflect on our behavior, acknowledge our mistakes, and make necessary adjustments. Taking ownership of our actions means recognizing that we are the architects of our own lives, and our decisions shape our future.

Personal responsibility also involves the ability to make informed choices and understand the implications of those choices. For example, in managing finances, responsibility means budgeting wisely, saving for the future, and avoiding unnecessary debt. In maintaining health, it means making conscious decisions about diet, exercise, and lifestyle habits. These aspects of responsibility are crucial for achieving long-term well-being and stability.

Moreover, personal responsibility extends to our mental and emotional well-being. It involves recognizing our emotional needs, seeking help when necessary, and taking proactive steps to manage stress and mental health. This aspect of responsibility is essential for maintaining a balanced and fulfilling life, as it empowers us to take control of our emotions and reactions rather than being overwhelmed by external circumstances.

Responsibility in Relationships

Responsibility extends to our interactions with others, where it plays a crucial role in building trust and maintaining healthy relationships. In relationships, being responsible means being reliable, keeping promises, and demonstrating consideration for others' needs and feelings. It involves acknowledging the impact of our actions on others and taking steps to address any negative consequences. Responsibility in relationships also means addressing conflicts constructively, being willing to communicate openly, and working collaboratively to resolve issues. This aspect of responsibility fosters mutual respect and support, which is essential for nurturing meaningful and enduring connections.

In family relationships, responsibility may involve caring for children, supporting a partner, or assisting aging parents. These responsibilities require a deep commitment and often involve making personal sacrifices for the well-being of loved ones. The ability to balance personal needs with the needs of others is a hallmark of mature responsibility in relationships.

In friendships and social interactions, responsibility involves being there for others in times of need, offering support and understanding, and maintaining honesty and integrity in communication. This helps to build trust and fosters long-lasting and meaningful connections. The responsibility in these relationships lies in contributing to a positive and supportive dynamic where all parties feel valued and respected.

Responsibility in Professional Settings

In professional settings, responsibility is equally important. It involves fulfilling job duties with competence and integrity, adhering to ethical standards, and contributing to a positive work environment. Professional responsibility requires taking ownership of our roles, being accountable for our performance, and striving for continuous improvement. It also involves managing responsibilities with diligence, addressing challenges proactively, and supporting colleagues and organizational goals. By demonstrating responsibility in the workplace, we build credibility, earn respect, and contribute to a culture of accountability and excellence.

Responsibility in the workplace also includes managing time effectively, meeting deadlines, and delivering quality work. It involves taking initiative, being proactive in solving problems, and being willing to take on additional tasks when needed. This level of responsibility is crucial for professional growth and advancement, as it demonstrates reliability and a strong work ethic.

Furthermore, professional responsibility extends to ethical behavior, such as maintaining confidentiality, avoiding conflicts of interest, and acting with honesty and integrity in all business dealings. This ethical dimension of responsibility is essential for building trust with clients, colleagues, and stakeholders and for upholding the reputation and values of the organization.

Social Responsibility and Ethical Considerations

The concept of responsibility is not only about individual actions but also about our broader social obligations. Social responsibility encompasses our role in contributing to the well-being of our communities and society at large. It involves advocating for justice, supporting initiatives that promote the common good, and making choices that reflect ethical considerations. Social responsibility requires an understanding of our impact on others and the environment and a commitment to addressing societal issues. This aspect of responsibility encourages active engagement in efforts to create positive change and improve the quality of life for others.

Social responsibility can manifest in various ways, such as volunteering, supporting charitable causes, and participating in community service. It also involves being mindful of the impact of our consumer choices, such as choosing sustainable products, reducing waste, and supporting ethical businesses. By embracing social responsibility, we contribute to the creation of a more just, equitable, and sustainable world.

Moreover, social responsibility extends to advocating for policies and practices that address social inequalities and injustices. This can involve participating in activism, supporting marginalized communities, and using our voices to promote positive change. It is about recognizing our role in shaping society and taking action to create a more inclusive and compassionate world.

Leadership and Responsibility

Responsibility also plays a crucial role in leadership. Effective leaders are defined by their ability to make informed decisions, guide others with integrity, and foster a culture of accountability. Leadership responsibility involves setting a positive example, navigating ethical dilemmas, and addressing challenges with transparency and fairness. It requires the courage to make tough decisions, the ability to inspire and motivate others, and a commitment to the greater good. Leaders who embrace responsibility build trust, inspire confidence, and create an environment where individuals feel empowered to take ownership of their roles and contribute to shared goals.

Responsible leadership also involves being accountable for the outcomes of decisions and actions, whether they result in success or failure. A responsible leader does not shift blame onto others but takes ownership of mistakes and works to correct them. This level of accountability builds credibility and trust within the organization and fosters a culture of learning and growth.

In addition, responsible leadership requires a commitment to ethical practices and social responsibility. Leaders are in a position to influence organizational values and behaviors, and their actions set the tone for the entire organization. By prioritizing ethical behavior, transparency, and social responsibility, leaders can create a positive impact both within and outside the organization.

Challenges in Embracing Responsibility

Embracing responsibility is not always straightforward, as it can present various challenges. External pressures, personal limitations, and conflicting values can make it difficult to navigate responsibilities effectively. Overcoming these challenges involves developing resilience, seeking support when needed, and maintaining a commitment to personal and professional growth. It requires the ability to manage stress, make difficult decisions, and stay true to one's values despite adversity.

One common challenge in embracing responsibility is the fear of failure. Taking responsibility often involves stepping out of one's comfort zone and facing the possibility of making mistakes. This fear can lead to avoidance or procrastination, preventing individuals from fully embracing their responsibilities. Overcoming this challenge requires a shift in mindset, recognizing that failure is a natural part of growth and learning and that taking responsibility is a sign of strength, not weakness.

Another challenge is balancing multiple responsibilities, especially in today's fast-paced and demanding world. Juggling personal, professional, and social responsibilities can be overwhelming, leading to stress and burnout. Developing effective time management skills, setting realistic goals, and prioritizing tasks are essential strategies for managing responsibilities effectively. It is also important to practice self-care and seek support from others when needed.

The Evolution of Responsibility

Responsibility is also a concept that evolves with our experiences and societal changes. As we progress through different stages of life and encounter new challenges, our sense of responsibility expands and adapts. This evolution requires continuous learning and adaptability, as well as a willingness to address emerging issues with foresight and integrity. The concept of responsibility extends to global challenges, such as climate change and inequality, where individuals and organizations must address collective concerns and contribute to solutions.

In the personal realm, our sense of responsibility evolves as we move through different life stages. For example, the responsibilities of a young adult just starting a career differ significantly from those of a parent raising children or a retiree managing their health and finances. As we encounter new challenges and opportunities, we must continuously reassess our responsibilities and adapt our behavior accordingly.

On a societal level, the concept of responsibility has evolved to encompass global challenges that require collective action. Issues such as climate change, social inequality, and public health demand a broader understanding of responsibility that goes beyond individual or organizational actions. Addressing these challenges requires a collaborative effort where individuals, businesses, and governments work together to create sustainable and equitable solutions.

The Role of Responsibility in Personal and Societal Functioning

Ultimately, responsibility is a key function of personal and societal functioning. It shapes how we approach our obligations, interact with others, and contribute to the greater good. Embracing responsibility is essential for personal growth, building trust in relationships, and driving positive change in society. It requires self-awareness, ethical judgment, and the ability to navigate challenges with integrity and perseverance.

Responsibility is fundamental to the functioning of society, as it ensures that individuals and organizations act in ways that are consistent with ethical principles and contribute to the common good. Without responsibility, social structures would break down, trust would erode, and progress would be hindered. By taking ownership of our actions and their consequences, we contribute to a more just, equitable, and sustainable world.

In conclusion, responsibility is a fundamental aspect of human life that influences every decision and action we take. It is the quality that guides us in managing our personal affairs, interacting with others, and contributing to the broader community. Responsibility is essential for personal growth, effective leadership, and fostering positive relationships. Despite the challenges associated with embracing responsibility, it is a critical component of living a purposeful and fulfilling life. By taking ownership of our actions and their consequences, we contribute positively to our own lives, the lives of others, and the world at large. Responsibility is not just a duty but an opportunity to make a meaningful impact and create a better future for ourselves and future generations.

CHAPTER 26
GENEROSITY

"We make a living by what we get. We make a life by what we give." — Winston Churchill

Generosity: The Timeless Virtue of Giving

Generosity is a quality that spans all ages, cultures, and situations, shedding light on the essence of human connection and empathy. It is a profound attribute that reflects the willingness to give of oneself, whether through material means, time, or kindness, without expecting anything in return. Generosity is not just an act but a mindset, a way of being that fosters goodwill and strengthens the fabric of society.

The Essence of Generosity

At its core, generosity is rooted in the understanding that we are all interconnected. When we give freely, we acknowledge our shared humanity and contribute to a collective sense of well-being. This selflessness enriches both the giver and the receiver, creating a ripple effect that extends far beyond the immediate act of giving. Generosity builds bridges, fosters relationships, and cultivates an environment where compassion thrives.

Generosity can manifest in countless ways, from small, everyday acts to grand gestures. Simple acts like offering a smile, lending a listening ear, or sharing a meal can have profound impacts on others. These seemingly minor gestures often hold the power to brighten someone's day, alleviate loneliness, or provide comfort in times of need. On a larger scale, acts of generosity might include donating to charitable causes, volunteering time and skills, or supporting community initiatives. Regardless of the scale, the underlying principle remains the same: giving with an open heart and a genuine desire to make a positive difference.

The Personal Growth and Fulfillment of Generosity

One of the most compelling aspects of generosity is its ability to foster personal growth and fulfillment. When individuals engage in acts of kindness, they often experience a sense of purpose and satisfaction that goes beyond the immediate benefits of their actions. Generosity can lead to increased happiness, a stronger sense of community, and a deeper understanding of one's values and priorities. The act of giving helps us to step outside of our own concerns and focus on the needs and well-being of others. This shift in perspective can lead to a more fulfilling and meaningful life.

Research supports the idea that generosity contributes to personal well-being. Studies have shown that people who engage in generous behaviors tend to report higher levels of life satisfaction and emotional well-being. This positive effect is often attributed to the release of endorphins, sometimes referred to as the "helper's high," which occurs when we perform acts of kindness. Additionally, generosity fosters a sense of connection and belonging, which are essential components of psychological health.

Generosity also challenges us to grow beyond our comfort zones. It often requires us to confront our fears, insecurities, and the instinctive desire to prioritize self-preservation. By practicing generosity, we learn to trust in the abundance of life and to develop a mindset of gratitude and openness. This growth in character not only enriches our lives but also enhances our ability to navigate challenges with resilience and grace.

The Impact of Generosity

Furthermore, generosity has the power to inspire and encourage others to act similarly. Acts of kindness and selflessness can create a ripple effect, motivating others to contribute to the collective good. This phenomenon is often observed in communities where generosity becomes a shared value, leading to a culture of mutual support and collaboration. When people see the positive impacts of generosity, they are more likely to engage in similar behaviors, amplifying the reach and effectiveness of compassionate actions.

This ripple effect of generosity is evident in social movements and community initiatives where collective action leads to significant change. When individuals come together to support a cause, the impact is often greater than the sum of its parts. This collective generosity can drive social progress, address injustices, and foster a sense of unity and purpose among diverse groups of people.

Generosity also fosters a culture of giving within organizations and institutions. Companies that prioritize corporate social responsibility and philanthropy often inspire their employees and stakeholders to engage in charitable activities. This organizational culture of generosity not only benefits the community but also enhances employee morale, loyalty, and overall job satisfaction.

Generosity as a Catalyst for Social Change

Generosity also plays a crucial role in addressing societal challenges and fostering social change. By giving generously, individuals and organizations can support causes that aim to improve conditions for marginalized or underserved populations. Philanthropy, charitable giving, and social activism are all expressions of generosity that can lead to significant advancements in areas such as education, healthcare, and environmental sustainability. Generosity fuels movements for social justice and equity, helping to address systemic issues and create a more just and compassionate world.

Philanthropy has a long history of driving social change. Many of the world's most significant advancements in education, health, and civil rights have been supported by the generous contributions of individuals and foundations. These acts of generosity have the power to transform societies, providing resources and opportunities to those in need and challenging the status quo.

In recent years, the rise of social entrepreneurship has further demonstrated the impact of generosity on social change. Social entrepreneurs use innovative business models to address social issues, often reinvesting profits into their communities or causes. This blending of business acumen and altruism exemplifies how generosity can be a powerful force for good in the modern world.

Generosity in Building Relationships and Community Bonds

In addition to its social and personal benefits, generosity can also enhance relationships and strengthen community bonds. When we give freely, we build trust and foster a sense of connection with others. Generosity can break down barriers and bridge divides, creating opportunities for collaboration and mutual support. It can transform interactions and relationships, leading to deeper and more meaningful connections. Whether in personal relationships or within a broader community, acts of generosity can contribute to a more cohesive and supportive environment.

Generosity in relationships is often expressed through acts of kindness, such as offering emotional support, sharing resources, or simply being present for someone in need. These acts of giving strengthen the bonds between individuals and create a foundation of trust and mutual respect. Over time, generosity in relationships leads to a deeper sense of connection and understanding, fostering a sense of security and belonging.

In communities, generosity plays a vital role in creating a sense of shared purpose and collective well-being. When community members engage in acts of generosity, whether through volunteering, supporting local businesses, or participating in community events, they contribute to a positive and inclusive environment. This communal generosity strengthens social ties, promotes civic engagement, and enhances the overall quality of life for all members of the community.

The Challenges and Rewards of Generosity

Despite its many benefits, generosity is not always easy. It requires vulnerability and the willingness to step outside of our comfort zones. It can be challenging to give without expecting anything in return, and it may require sacrifices of time, resources, or personal comfort. However, these challenges are often outweighed by the rewards of making a positive impact and fostering connections with others.

One of the significant challenges of practicing generosity is overcoming the fear of scarcity—the belief that there is not enough to go around. This mindset can lead to hoarding resources, whether material or emotional, out of fear that we will be left with nothing. Generosity, on the other hand, is based on a mindset of abundance, the belief that by giving, we create more value for ourselves and others.

Another challenge is the societal emphasis on individualism and self-reliance, which can sometimes discourage acts of generosity. In cultures that prioritize personal achievement and success, generosity may be seen as a sign of weakness or as something that detracts from one's resources or opportunities. Overcoming these societal norms requires a conscious effort to value generosity as a strength and to recognize the long-term benefits of a giving mindset.

Cultivating Generosity

To cultivate generosity, individuals can start by reflecting on their own values and priorities. Understanding what truly matters to us can help guide our actions and decisions regarding how we give. It is also important to recognize and challenge any barriers that may hinder our ability to be generous, such as fear, insecurity, or self-doubt. By addressing these obstacles and embracing a mindset of abundance and compassion, we can enhance our capacity to give and contribute to the well-being of others.

Cultivating generosity also involves developing habits of giving in everyday life. This can include small acts of kindness, such as helping a neighbor, supporting a friend in need, or donating to a charitable cause. Over time, these habits of giving become ingrained in our daily routines, making generosity a natural and integral part of our lives.

Mindfulness and gratitude practices can also support the cultivation of generosity. By regularly reflecting on the things we are grateful for, we become more aware of the abundance in our lives and more inclined to share that abundance with others. This awareness helps to shift our focus from what we lack to what we can give, fostering a spirit of generosity and openness.

Generosity in Practice: Real-World Examples

Generosity is a transformative force that has the power to shape our lives and our world. It is a reflection of our shared humanity and a testament to our capacity for compassion and empathy. Through acts of kindness, selflessness, and support, we can create a more connected, caring, and equitable world. Generosity enriches our lives, strengthens our communities, and drives positive change, reminding us of the profound impact we can have when we give from the heart.

One example of generosity in action is the story of philanthropists like Warren Buffett and Bill Gates, who have pledged to give away a significant portion of their wealth to address global issues such as poverty, health, and education. Their commitment to philanthropy has inspired other wealthy individuals to join the Giving Pledge, a campaign that encourages billionaires to contribute the majority of their wealth to charitable causes. This movement has the potential to create significant positive change in the world, demonstrating the power of generosity on a large scale.

On a smaller scale, the everyday acts of generosity that occur within communities are equally impactful. For example, local food banks, supported by donations from individuals and businesses, provide essential resources to families in need. Community gardens, often maintained by volunteers, offer fresh produce to residents and create opportunities for social interaction and collaboration. These acts of generosity contribute to the overall health and well-being of the community, fostering a sense of solidarity and mutual support.

The Legacy of Generosity

In conclusion, generosity is a foundational element of a compassionate and thriving society. It embodies the principles of selflessness, empathy, and connection, enriching both the giver and the receiver. By embracing generosity, we contribute to the greater good, build meaningful relationships, and foster positive social change. As we navigate our lives, let us remember the power of generosity and strive to infuse it into our actions, creating an impact that resonates far beyond our immediate reach. Through the simple yet profound act of giving, we can make a lasting impact on the world and inspire others to do the same.

The legacy of generosity is not only in the tangible outcomes of our actions but also in the example we set for future generations. By practicing generosity, we model values of kindness, compassion, and community for our children and others who look up to us. This legacy of giving can inspire others to continue the cycle of generosity, creating a culture where giving and sharing are valued and celebrated.

Generosity, in its many forms, has the power to transform lives, communities, and the world. It is a quality that reflects the best of humanity and serves as a reminder of the profound connections that unite us all. Whether through small acts of kindness or grand philanthropic efforts, the impact of generosity is far-reaching and enduring. As we continue to embrace and practice generosity, we contribute to a more just, compassionate, and connected world, leaving a lasting legacy of goodwill and positive change.

CHAPTER 27
GRATITUDE

"Gratitude is when memory is stored in the heart and not in the mind." — Lionel Hampton

Gratitude: A Pathway to Fulfillment and Well-Being

Gratitude deeply enriches our daily lives, acting as a powerful force that permeates our daily lives, offering a lens through which we can appreciate the richness and beauty of our existence. At its core, gratitude is the recognition and acknowledgment of the goodness in our lives, and it involves a deep sense of thankfulness for the people, experiences, and opportunities that contribute to our well-being. This simple yet powerful emotion can have far-reaching effects on our mental, emotional, and physical health, as well as on our relationships and overall quality of life.

The Spirit of Gratitude

To understand gratitude fully, it is important to recognize that it is more than just a fleeting feeling or a polite response. Gratitude is a deliberate and intentional practice that involves consciously reflecting on and appreciating the positive aspects of life. It is an attitude that invites us to shift our focus from what is lacking or problematic to what is already present and valuable. This shift in perspective fosters a sense of contentment and joy, even in the face of adversity or challenge.

Gratitude is not simply about saying "thank you" in response to kindness; it is about cultivating a mindset that consistently recognizes and values the good in our lives. It requires us to pause and reflect, to acknowledge the contributions of others, and to appreciate the beauty and wonder of the world around us. This practice of gratitude deepens our awareness of the interconnectedness of life and enhances our ability to experience joy and fulfillment in everyday moments.

Gratitude and Mental Well-Being

One of the most significant benefits of practicing gratitude is its impact on our mental and emotional well-being. Research has shown that individuals who regularly engage in gratitude practices, such as keeping a gratitude journal or expressing thanks to others, experience higher levels of happiness and life satisfaction. Gratitude helps to counteract negative emotions like envy, resentment, and frustration by redirecting our attention to the positive aspects of our lives. This positive focus can enhance our overall mood and contribute to a greater sense of inner peace and resilience.

Gratitude also has a unique ability to shift our mindset from one of scarcity to one of abundance. When we focus on what we are grateful for, we become more aware of the abundance in our lives, reducing feelings of lack or insufficiency. This shift in perspective can lead to greater optimism and a more positive outlook on life, even during challenging times. By focusing on what we have rather than what we lack, gratitude fosters a sense of contentment and helps us to appreciate the present moment.

The Role of Gratitude in connections

Gratitude plays a crucial role in strengthening our relationships and fostering social connections. When we express appreciation and thanks to others, we not only acknowledge their contributions but also affirm the value of our relationship with them. Acts of gratitude, whether through a heartfelt thank-you note, a kind gesture, or a simple verbal expression, can deepen bonds, build trust, and enhance mutual respect. In this way, gratitude serves as a catalyst for creating and maintaining meaningful connections with others.

Gratitude also encourages us to focus on the positive qualities of others, which can improve our interactions and reduce conflict. By recognizing and appreciating the good in others, we are more likely to respond with kindness, empathy, and understanding. This positive reinforcement strengthens relationships and creates a supportive and nurturing environment where everyone feels valued and appreciated.

In addition, gratitude can play a pivotal role in resolving conflicts and repairing strained relationships. When we approach others with gratitude, we are more likely to listen actively, express empathy, and seek common ground. This attitude fosters open communication and mutual understanding, which are essential for resolving disagreements and building stronger, more resilient relationships.

Gratitude and Physical Health

The practice of gratitude can have a positive impact on our physical health as well. Studies have found that individuals who regularly practice gratitude experience lower levels of stress, reduced symptoms of depression, and improved sleep quality. Gratitude has been linked to lower blood pressure and a stronger immune system, which can contribute to overall better health. The act of acknowledging and appreciating the positive aspects of our lives promotes a healthier and more balanced lifestyle, enhancing our overall well-being.

One explanation for the link between gratitude and physical health is the reduction of stress. Chronic stress has been shown to have numerous negative effects on the body, including increased risk of heart disease, weakened immune function, and disrupted sleep patterns. By practicing gratitude, we reduce our stress levels and promote relaxation, which can have a direct impact on our physical health.

Moreover, gratitude encourages us to take better care of ourselves. When we appreciate our bodies and the lives we have, we are more likely to engage in healthy behaviors, such as regular exercise, balanced nutrition, and adequate rest. This self-care not only improves our physical health but also enhances our overall sense of well-being and vitality.

Gratitude and Mindfulness

Gratitude is closely connected to the concept of mindfulness, which involves being fully present and aware of the present moment. By practicing gratitude, we cultivate a mindful awareness of the positive aspects of our lives, allowing us to fully experience and savor the richness of each moment. This mindful approach to gratitude can enhance our ability to appreciate the beauty and value in everyday experiences, fostering a deeper sense of fulfillment and contentment.

Mindfulness and gratitude complement each other in powerful ways. Mindfulness encourages us to slow down and notice the details of our lives, while gratitude helps us to appreciate those details. Together, they create a positive feedback loop that enhances our awareness, deepens our appreciation, and fosters a greater sense of peace and well-being.

For example, when we practice mindful gratitude, we may take a moment to fully appreciate the taste of a meal, the warmth of the sun on our skin, or the sound of a loved one's voice. By focusing our attention on these experiences and expressing gratitude for them, we deepen our connection to the present moment and enhance our overall sense of joy and fulfillment.

Gratitude's Broader Societal Impact

In addition to its personal benefits, gratitude can also have a broader societal impact. When practiced collectively, gratitude can contribute to the creation of a more compassionate and supportive community. By fostering an environment where appreciation and kindness are valued, gratitude can encourage positive social interactions and promote a culture of mutual support and empathy. In this way, gratitude has the potential to enhance social cohesion and contribute to the overall well-being of society.

A society that values gratitude is one where individuals are more likely to help and support one another, creating a sense of community and shared responsibility. This collective sense of gratitude can lead to greater social harmony, reduced conflict, and increased cooperation. It can also inspire acts of kindness and generosity, which then spread outward, impacting more than just individual interactions and enriching the wider community.

Gratitude can also play a role in addressing social and environmental issues. When we practice gratitude for the natural world and the resources it provides, we are more likely to take action to protect and preserve it. Similarly, when we express gratitude for the contributions of others, we are more likely to support efforts to promote social justice and equality. In this way, gratitude can inspire positive change and contribute to the creation of a more just and sustainable world.

Cultivating Gratitude in Challenging Times

Despite its many benefits, gratitude is not always easy to cultivate, especially in challenging or difficult times. It can be easy to focus on what is going wrong or to become overwhelmed by negative circumstances. However, even in the midst of adversity, there are opportunities to practice gratitude and find moments of appreciation. By intentionally seeking out and acknowledging the positive aspects of our lives, we can build resilience and maintain a hopeful perspective, even in the face of difficulties.

Cultivating gratitude in challenging times requires a conscious effort to shift our focus from what is lacking to what is present and valuable. This may involve identifying small moments of joy, such as a kind word from a friend or a beautiful sunset, and expressing gratitude for them. It may also involve reflecting on the strengths and resources we have that help us navigate difficult situations.

One powerful way to cultivate gratitude in challenging times is through the practice of reframing. Reframing involves looking at a difficult situation from a different perspective and finding the positive aspects within it. For example, instead of focusing on the inconvenience of being stuck in traffic, we might express gratitude for the opportunity to listen to a favorite podcast or reflect on our day. By reframing our experiences in this way, we can transform challenges into opportunities for growth and appreciation.

The Transformative Power of Gratitude

In conclusion, gratitude is a powerful quality that enriches our lives and enhances our overall well-being. It involves a deliberate and intentional practice of recognizing and appreciating the positive aspects of our lives, and it has far-reaching effects on our mental, emotional, and physical health. By fostering a practice of gratitude, we can strengthen our relationships, enhance our quality of life, and contribute to a more compassionate and supportive society.

Gratitude is not just an emotion; it is a way of being that shapes how we see the world and interact with others. It encourages us to focus on the good, to appreciate the small blessings in life, and to express our thanks freely and generously. Through the practice of gratitude, we can create a environment that not only transforms our own lives but also touches the lives of those around us.

As we navigate our lives, let us remember the profound impact of gratitude and strive to cultivate it in our daily experiences. By doing so, we can create a richer, more fulfilling life for ourselves and contribute to the well-being of others. Gratitude is a gift that keeps on giving, and by embracing it, we can truly appreciate the beauty and abundance that life has to offer.

CHAPTER 28
COMPASSION

"The best way to find yourself is to lose yourself in the service of others." — Mahatma Gandhi

Compassion: A Pillar of Humanity

Compassion is the ability to empathize with the suffering of others and to take action to alleviate that suffering. This quality transcends mere sympathy, as it involves a deeper emotional connection and a genuine desire to help those in need. Compassion is not just a passive feeling but an active response to the challenges and difficulties faced by others. It manifests in both grand gestures and small acts of kindness, each contributing to the greater good of humanity.

At its core, compassion is about recognizing the shared human experience of pain and joy. It is an acknowledgment that despite our individual differences, we all experience moments of vulnerability and hardship. This recognition fosters a sense of solidarity and understanding, encouraging us to reach out and support one another. Compassion is the force that motivates us to act selflessly, to put the needs of others before our own, and to work towards creating a more just and equitable world.

One of the most compelling aspects of compassion is its transformative power. When we practice compassion, we not only help others but also enrich our own lives. Acts of compassion can lead to a greater sense of fulfillment and purpose as they connect us to something larger than ourselves. By extending kindness and support to others, we cultivate a sense of belonging and connection that enhances our overall well-being. This reciprocal relationship highlights the profound impact that compassion can have on both individuals and communities.

The Modern Relevance of Compassion

In modern times, the value of compassion remains just as relevant. Studies have shown that compassionate behavior can have significant positive effects on mental and physical health. For instance, research has found that individuals who engage in acts of kindness and generosity experience lower levels of stress and anxiety. Additionally, compassionate actions can lead to improved relationships and a greater sense of community. These findings underscore the importance of cultivating compassion in our daily lives, as it contributes to both personal and collective well-being.

The modern world, with its fast-paced lifestyle and technological advancements, can often create a sense of disconnection and isolation. In such an environment, compassion serves as a vital counterbalance, reminding us of our shared humanity and the importance of empathy and understanding. Whether it is through volunteering, supporting charitable causes, or simply offering a listening ear to a friend in need, acts of compassion help to bridge the gaps that can arise in a fragmented society.

Compassion also plays a crucial role in addressing social and global issues. In the face of challenges such as poverty, inequality, and conflict, compassionate responses can drive meaningful change. Organizations and individuals dedicated to humanitarian efforts often rely on compassion as a guiding principle. By fostering empathy and understanding, they work towards creating solutions that address the root causes of suffering and promote social justice. This compassionate approach can lead to more sustainable and impactful outcomes, as it prioritizes the needs and voices of those most affected.

For example, global movements for social justice, such as the fight for disability rights or the efforts to combat climate change, are often driven by a deep sense of compassion for those who are most vulnerable. These movements recognize that true change can only come about when we address the underlying causes of suffering and work towards a more just and equitable world.

Cultivating Compassion in Daily Life

Cultivating compassion is not without its challenges. In a world marked by division and conflict, it can be difficult to maintain a compassionate mindset. Prejudices, misunderstandings, and societal pressures can create barriers to empathy and understanding. Despite these obstacles, it is essential to persevere in our efforts to practice compassion. By actively seeking to understand others' perspectives and addressing our own biases, we can overcome these barriers and build a more inclusive and empathetic society.

One of the key steps in cultivating compassion is developing self-awareness and emotional intelligence. By becoming more attuned to our own emotions and reactions, we can better understand the emotions and needs of others. This self-awareness allows us to respond with empathy and kindness rather than reacting out of frustration or anger. Mindfulness practices, such as meditation or deep breathing, can help to enhance self-awareness and create a sense of inner calm that supports compassionate behavior.

Another important aspect of cultivating compassion is practicing active listening. When we listen to others with an open mind and a genuine desire to understand their experiences, we create a space for empathy and connection to flourish. Active listening involves not only hearing the words being spoken but also paying attention to the emotions and intentions behind those words. By listening deeply and responding with empathy, we can build stronger, more meaningful relationships.

Compassion also requires a commitment to self-care. It is important to recognize that we cannot pour from an empty cup; taking care of our own well-being is essential for sustaining our ability to help others. Practicing self-compassion and setting healthy boundaries allows us to maintain our emotional and physical health, enabling us to continue offering support and kindness to those in need.

In addition to these personal practices, there are numerous opportunities to cultivate compassion on a broader scale. Volunteering with local organizations, supporting social justice initiatives, and advocating for policies that promote equity and inclusion are all ways to extend compassion beyond our immediate circles. By engaging in these efforts, we contribute to creating a more compassionate and just society.

The Compassion of Mother Teresa

Mother Teresa, one of the most iconic figures of the 20th century, dedicated her life to helping the poorest of the poor in the slums of Calcutta, India. Despite the difficult conditions and limited resources, she founded the Missionaries of Charity and worked tirelessly to provide care for those in need. Her selfless acts of kindness and her unwavering commitment to serving others have inspired countless individuals to pursue lives of compassion and service. Mother Teresa's legacy is a powerful reminder of the impact that one person's love and dedication can have on the world.

Mother Teresa's approach to compassion was grounded in her deep spiritual beliefs and her commitment to seeing the divine in every person. She often spoke of the importance of loving others as we love ourselves and of recognizing the dignity and worth of every human being, regardless of their circumstances. Her compassion extended not only to those in dire need but also to her fellow sisters and the volunteers who worked alongside her. She believed that compassion was not just about grand gestures but about the small, everyday acts of kindness that make a difference in people's lives.

The Effect of Compassion

No matter what challenges we face, the human spirit has the capacity to rise above adversity, dream big, and create lasting change. Every individual, through their unique journey, has the ability to leave an indelible mark on the world, showing us that inspiration can come from perseverance, creativity, compassion, and the unwavering belief in a better future.

The effect of compassion can be seen in the countless acts of kindness and generosity that are inspired by these examples. When we witness or experience compassion, we are often moved to act in kind, spreading the positive impact even further. This ripple effect creates a chain of compassion that can transform communities and even entire societies.

Compassion has the power to break down barriers and foster understanding between people from different backgrounds, cultures, and experiences. It can heal divisions and bring people together in the pursuit of common goals. By cultivating compassion in our own lives and encouraging it in others, we contribute to creating a world that is more just, equitable, and humane.

Compassion as a Pathway to Global Peace

In the context of global challenges such as conflict, inequality, and environmental degradation, compassion offers a pathway to peace and sustainability. When we approach these challenges with compassion, we prioritize the well-being of all people and the planet, recognizing that our fates are interconnected. Compassion motivates us to seek solutions that address the root causes of suffering and that promote healing and reconciliation.

In conflict resolution, for example, compassion allows us to move beyond blame and retribution to seek understanding and common ground. By empathizing with the experiences and perspectives of others, we can work towards solutions that are fair and inclusive. This compassionate approach to conflict resolution has been successfully employed in various contexts, from international peace negotiations to community mediation efforts.

Similarly, in addressing global inequality, compassion drives us to advocate for policies and practices that uplift marginalized communities and that create opportunities for all people to thrive. By recognizing the systemic barriers that contribute to inequality, we can work towards creating a more just and equitable world.

The Enduring Impact of Compassion

Compassion is an essential and life-altering attribute that enriches our lives and strengthens our connections with others. It is the ability to empathize with and respond to the suffering of others, fostering a sense of solidarity and mutual support. Through acts of kindness, understanding, and generosity, we can create a more compassionate world, addressing both individual and collective needs. While cultivating compassion may present challenges, its benefits are profound and far-reaching. By embracing and practicing compassion, we contribute to a more just, empathetic, and harmonious society.

We can incorporate this quality into our daily lives. Whether through small acts of kindness, supporting those in need, or advocating for social justice, each of us has the power to make a difference. By choosing compassion, we not only improve our own lives but also contribute to the greater good, creating a world where empathy, kindness, and understanding prevail.

In the words of the Dalai Lama, "If you want others to be happy, practice compassion. If you want to be happy, practice compassion." This simple yet profound truth reminds us that compassion is not only something that we give to others but also a source of deep fulfillment and joy in our own lives.

CHAPTER 29
RESPECT

"I'm not concerned with your liking or disliking me... All I ask is that you respect me as a human being." – Jackie Robinson

Respect: The Foundation of Human Dignity and Social Harmony

Respect is a fundamental value that underpins human interaction, social cohesion, and individual integrity. It is a multifaceted concept that encompasses recognition of others' rights, consideration of others' feelings, and acknowledgment of others' worth. Respect is essential for building and maintaining healthy relationships, fostering social harmony, and ensuring that everyone is treated with dignity and fairness. This essay explores the nature of respect, its significance, the different forms it can take, and the challenges of practicing respect in various aspects of life.

Respect is the acknowledgment of the inherent worth and dignity of others. It involves treating people with consideration, valuing their rights, feelings, and opinions, and recognizing their humanity. Respect is not merely about politeness or social etiquette; it is a deeper ethical principle that guides our interactions and shapes our relationships with others.

At its core, respect is about recognizing the value of others and treating them accordingly. It involves seeing others as equals, deserving of the same rights, freedoms, and opportunities as ourselves. Respect is not about agreeing with others or condoning their behavior; rather, it is about acknowledging their humanity and treating them with the dignity they deserve.

Respect can be both an attitude and an action. As an attitude, it involves holding others in high regard and valuing their perspectives, even when they differ from our own. As an action, it involves behaving in ways that reflect this attitude, such as listening attentively, being considerate of others' needs, and refraining from harmful behavior.

Interactions With Respect

Respect can be understood in several dimensions, each of which plays a critical role in our interactions with others. Self-respect is the foundation of all forms of respect. It involves recognizing and honoring one's own worth and dignity. It includes having a healthy sense of self-esteem, setting boundaries, and maintaining one's integrity. Without self-respect, it is difficult to respect others genuinely.

Mutual respect is the reciprocal recognition of each other's value and dignity in relationships. It is essential for building trust, cooperation, and harmony between individuals. In a relationship characterized by mutual respect, both parties honor each other's rights, feelings, and needs.

Respect for authority involves acknowledging the legitimacy and responsibility of those in positions of authority, whether they are teachers, parents, managers, or public officials. Respecting authority is essential for maintaining order and structure in various social settings. However, it is important to note that respect for authority should be balanced with critical thinking and ethical considerations.

Cultural respect involves appreciating and honoring the beliefs, traditions, and practices of different cultures. In a world that is increasingly interconnected, cultural respect is vital for fostering understanding and peaceful coexistence among diverse communities.

Respect for nature involves recognizing the intrinsic value of the environment and all living beings. It is about understanding our interconnectedness with the natural world and taking responsibility for its preservation and protection.

Respect: The Big Picture

Respect is not just a social nicety; it is a cornerstone of ethical and moral behavior. The significance of respect can be seen in various aspects of life, including relationships, social cohesion, and personal growth.

Respect is the glue that holds relationships together. Whether it is a friendship, a romantic relationship, or a professional partnership, respect is essential for trust, communication, and mutual understanding. In relationships where respect is lacking, misunderstandings, conflicts, and resentment can quickly arise.

In a broader societal context, respect plays a crucial role in promoting social cohesion and harmony. When individuals and groups respect each other's differences—be it in terms of culture, religion, race, or ideology—it fosters an environment of tolerance and peace. In contrast, a lack of respect can lead to division, conflict, and even violence.

Respecting others' rights and freedoms, including freedom of speech, belief, and association, is fundamental to a just and democratic society. It allows for constructive dialogue, collaboration, and the peaceful resolution of differences.

Respect Related to Growth and Development

Respect is also essential for personal growth and development. When we respect ourselves and others, we create a positive environment that encourages learning, creativity, and self-expression. Respecting others' ideas and contributions can lead to innovation and progress, as diverse perspectives are valued and integrated.

Furthermore, respect for oneself fosters a healthy self-image and confidence, which are crucial for pursuing personal goals and aspirations. When we respect our own time, energy, and needs, we are better able to take care of ourselves and live fulfilling lives.

Human Dignity

Respect is intrinsically tied to the concept of human dignity—the belief that every person has inherent worth and deserves to be treated with honor and consideration. Upholding human dignity is a moral imperative that requires us to respect the rights and freedoms of others, regardless of their background, status, or circumstances.

In many human rights frameworks, respect for human dignity is a central principle. It underlies the idea that all individuals should be free from discrimination, violence, and oppression. By respecting human dignity, we contribute to a world where justice, equality, and human rights are upheld.

The Challenges of Respect

While respect is a universally valued principle, practicing it can sometimes be challenging. It requires self-awareness, empathy, and a commitment to ethical behavior. Effective communication is key to demonstrating respect. This involves not only the words we use but also our tone, body language, and listening skills. Respectful communication means being mindful of how our words and actions impact others, avoiding harmful language, and being open to different viewpoints.

Active listening is a critical component of respectful communication. It involves giving our full attention to the speaker, acknowledging their feelings and perspectives, and responding thoughtfully. By listening actively, we show that we value the other person's input and are willing to engage in a meaningful dialogue.

Respecting boundaries is another crucial aspect of practicing respect. Personal boundaries are the limits we set for ourselves in terms of what we are comfortable with, both physically and emotionally. Respecting these boundaries means not overstepping them and being considerate of others' comfort levels.

In the workplace, respecting professional boundaries is crucial for maintaining a healthy and productive environment. This includes respecting colleagues' time, privacy, and roles. By honoring boundaries, we create a space where everyone feels safe, respected, and valued.

Empathy is the ability to understand and share the feelings of others. It is a key ingredient in practicing respect, as it allows us to connect with others on a deeper level and appreciate their experiences. Empathy involves putting ourselves in others' shoes, considering how they might feel, and responding with kindness and compassion.

Respect and Fairness

By practicing empathy, we can better understand the impact of our actions on others and make more respectful choices. Empathy also helps us navigate conflicts and disagreements with greater sensitivity and care. Leaders play a pivotal role in setting the tone for respect within organizations and communities. Respectful leadership involves treating team members with fairness, valuing their contributions, and providing support and guidance. A respectful leader fosters an inclusive environment where everyone feels heard and appreciated.

Respectful leaders also lead by example, demonstrating integrity, accountability, and humility in their actions. By modeling respect, leaders can inspire others to follow suit and create a culture of respect within their organizations. In a diverse and interconnected world, cultural respect is more important than ever. This involves recognizing and appreciating the richness of different cultures, traditions, and perspectives. Cultivating cultural respect means being open to learning about other cultures, avoiding stereotypes and prejudices, and honoring the customs and practices of others.

Cultural respect also involves acknowledging the historical and social contexts that shape people's experiences. By understanding these contexts, we can engage more thoughtfully and respectfully with others from different backgrounds. Respect for nature is an essential aspect of ethical living. It involves recognizing the intrinsic value of the natural world and taking responsibility for its preservation. This includes making environmentally conscious choices, such as reducing waste, conserving resources, and supporting sustainable practices.

Respecting nature also means acknowledging the interconnectedness of all living beings and understanding our role in the ecosystem. By treating the environment with care and consideration, we contribute to the well-being of the planet and future generations.

Self Awareness

Despite its importance, respect is not always easy to practice. There are several challenges that can hinder the cultivation of respect in our lives. Prejudice and discrimination are significant barriers to respect. They involve negative attitudes and behaviors towards individuals or groups based on characteristics such as race, gender, religion, or nationality. Prejudice and discrimination can lead to disrespectful treatment, exclusion, and even violence.

Overcoming these challenges requires self-awareness, education, and a commitment to fairness and equality. It involves challenging our biases, confronting discriminatory behaviors, and advocating for the rights and dignity of all people. Power dynamics can also affect the practice of respect. In situations where there is an imbalance of power, such as in hierarchical organizations or social structures, those with more power may struggle to show respect to those with less. This can lead to exploitation, marginalization, and abuse.

Addressing power dynamics requires a conscious effort to recognize and challenge power imbalances. It involves creating systems and practices that promote equity, transparency, and accountability, ensuring that everyone is treated with respect and dignity. Conflicts and disagreements are inevitable in human interactions, and they can pose a challenge to respect. In heated situations, emotions can run high, leading to disrespectful behaviors such as name-calling, shouting, or dismissiveness.

Managing conflicts with respect involves maintaining a calm and open-minded approach, focusing on the issue at hand rather than attacking the person. It requires active listening, empathy, and a willingness to find common ground or agree to disagree. In our increasingly globalized world, cultural differences can sometimes lead to misunderstandings and a lack of respect. Practicing cultural respect involves being open to learning about other cultures, avoiding stereotypes, and honoring the customs and practices of others.

Despite these challenges, respect extends beyond individual interactions. When respect is practiced consistently, it fosters a sense of community, encourages collaboration, and creates an environment where everyone feels valued and supported. Communities built on respect are more resilient, cohesive, and capable of overcoming challenges.

Respect is a value that is passed down through generations. When children observe respectful behavior from adults, they are more likely to adopt these practices in their own lives. By modeling respect, we not only improve our own interactions but also contribute to a more respectful and empathetic future.

Practicing respect is not just about how we treat others; it also has a profound impact on our own personal growth and fulfillment. Respectful behavior leads to stronger relationships, greater self-esteem, and a more positive outlook on life. By embracing respect as a core value, we enrich our lives and the lives of those around us.

The Essence of Respect

In conclusion, respect is a fundamental aspect of human interaction that plays a crucial role in building healthy relationships, promoting social harmony, and upholding human dignity. It is a value that requires conscious effort to cultivate and maintain, especially in a world filled with challenges and differences. By practicing respect in our daily lives—through our communication, empathy, and interactions with others—we can create a more inclusive, understanding, and compassionate world. Respect is not just a social nicety; it is a powerful force that can transform individuals, relationships, and entire communities.

CHAPTER 30
HUMILITY

"It is not the mountain we conquer, but ourselves."

— Sir Edmund Hillary

Humility: The Foundation of Personal Growth

Humility is an often misunderstood quality that plays a crucial role in personal growth, relationships, and leadership. At its core, humility is the ability to recognize and accept one's limitations, weaknesses, and imperfections while valuing the strengths and contributions of others. It is not about self-deprecation or diminishing one's own worth but rather about maintaining a balanced perspective that allows for genuine connection and continuous learning.

Understanding Humility

One of the most important aspects of humility is the capacity for self-awareness. Humble individuals possess a clear understanding of their strengths and weaknesses, and they do not let their accomplishments inflate their self-worth. They recognize that while they may have certain talents or skills, they are not infallible and have areas where they can grow. This self-awareness fosters a sense of openness to feedback and constructive criticism, which is essential for personal and professional development.

Humility is also about embracing one's imperfections and being comfortable with vulnerability. It involves acknowledging that no one is perfect and that making mistakes is a natural part of the human experience. Rather than hiding or denying their flaws, humble individuals are willing to confront them openly and learn from them. This attitude not only enhances personal growth but also fosters a more authentic and supportive environment in relationships and workplaces.

Humility in Personal Growth

Humility is fundamental to personal growth because it allows individuals to see themselves clearly without the distortions of ego or pride. When we are humble, we are more likely to acknowledge our need for improvement and seek out opportunities for learning and development. This willingness to learn and grow is a key driver of personal and professional success.

For example, in the pursuit of knowledge, humility manifests as intellectual humility—a recognition that our understanding of the world is limited and that we must remain open to new ideas and perspectives. This openness to learning prevents the stagnation of thought and encourages the continuous development of skills and understanding. Intellectual humility allows individuals to engage in lifelong learning, adapt to changing circumstances, and remain curious about the world around them.

Humility also enhances emotional intelligence, which is crucial for navigating the complexities of human relationships. By recognizing our own emotions and how they influence our behavior, we can better understand the emotions of others. This emotional awareness fosters empathy and compassion, allowing us to connect with others on a deeper level and respond to their needs with kindness and understanding.

Humility in Relationships

In the realm of relationships, humility is the foundation of deep connections and trust. Humble individuals approach their interactions with a genuine curiosity about others, valuing their experiences and perspectives. This approach creates a space for open and honest communication where both parties feel heard and respected.

When individuals approach relationships with humility, they are more likely to listen actively, validate others' experiences, and offer support without judgment. This active listening is essential for building trust and understanding, as it shows that we value the other person's thoughts and feelings. In contrast, a lack of humility can lead to misunderstandings, conflicts, and a breakdown in communication.

Humility also plays a crucial role in conflict resolution. In disagreements, humble individuals are more likely to seek common ground and approach the situation with a willingness to compromise. They recognize that they may not have all the answers and are open to considering different perspectives. This openness and flexibility can lead to more effective and lasting resolutions, as both parties feel respected and valued.

Furthermore, humility in relationships fosters a sense of equality and mutual respect. By valuing the strengths and contributions of others, humble individuals create an environment where everyone feels appreciated and empowered. This mutual respect is the foundation of strong and enduring relationships, whether in personal life, friendships, or professional settings.

Humility in Leadership

Humility is also a cornerstone of effective leadership. Great leaders often exhibit humility by putting the needs of their team before their own. They listen to others, value their input, and are willing to share credit for successes. Humble leaders are approachable and willing to admit when they do not have all the answers, which creates a culture of trust and openness. This type of leadership inspires others to contribute their best and fosters a sense of collective purpose and achievement.

Humble leaders understand that leadership is not about asserting authority or control but about serving others and guiding them toward a common goal. This servant leadership approach is characterized by empathy, active listening, and a focus on the well-being of the team. By prioritizing the needs and development of their team members, humble leaders create an environment where individuals feel supported, valued, and motivated to perform at their best.

Moreover, humility in leadership is essential for fostering innovation and adaptability. Humble leaders are open to new ideas and are willing to take calculated risks. They encourage creativity and experimentation within their teams, recognizing that failure is a natural part of the innovation process. By creating space for exploration and learning, humble leaders empower their teams to think outside the box and drive continuous improvement.

Humility as a Key to Resilience

Humility is a key component of resilience, the ability to bounce back from adversity and continue moving forward. The ability to remain grounded and focused, even in the face of adversity, is a hallmark of resilient individuals. Humility allows individuals to accept and adapt to challenges without becoming overwhelmed by ego or pride. It helps them to view setbacks as opportunities for growth and to approach difficulties with a sense of grace and perseverance.

When faced with challenges, humble individuals are more likely to seek support and guidance from others. They recognize that they do not have to face adversity alone and are open to receiving help and advice. This willingness to lean on others strengthens their resilience and allows them to navigate difficult situations more effectively.

Humility also fosters a growth mindset, which is crucial for resilience. A growth mindset is the belief that abilities and intelligence can be developed through effort, learning, and perseverance. Humble individuals embrace this mindset, viewing challenges as opportunities to learn and grow rather than as threats to their self-worth. This perspective allows them to persevere through difficulties and emerge stronger on the other side.

The Misconceptions of Humility

Despite its many benefits, humility is often misunderstood and undervalued. In a culture that often emphasizes individual achievement and self-promotion, humility can be seen as a weakness or a lack of confidence. However, true humility is not about downplaying one's abilities or achievements but rather about maintaining a balanced perspective that allows for growth, collaboration, and authentic connections.

One common misconception is that humility involves thinking less of oneself or diminishing one's accomplishments. However, humility is not about self-deprecation but about having an accurate and balanced view of oneself. It involves recognizing one's strengths and contributions while also acknowledging areas for improvement and valuing the strengths of others. This balanced perspective allows for genuine self-confidence and self-respect, which are essential for personal growth and fulfillment.

Another misconception is that humility is incompatible with ambition or success. However, many successful individuals attribute their achievements to a combination of hard work, talent, and humility. Humility allows individuals to remain open to feedback, learn from their experiences, and build strong relationships—all of which are crucial for long-term success. In fact, humility can be a powerful driver of success, as it fosters continuous learning and improvement.

Cultivating Humility

Cultivating humility involves a conscious effort to shift one's mindset and behaviors. It requires self-reflection, a willingness to confront one's limitations, and a commitment to valuing and respecting others. Practices such as mindfulness, active listening, and seeking feedback can help individuals develop and strengthen their sense of humility. Additionally, surrounding oneself with diverse perspectives and engaging in acts of service can further enhance one's appreciation for the strengths and contributions of others.

Mindfulness, the practice of being present and fully engaged at the moment, is a powerful tool for cultivating humility. Mindfulness helps individuals to observe their thoughts and emotions without judgment, allowing them to gain insight into their own behaviors and motivations. This self-awareness is the foundation of humility, as it enables individuals to recognize their strengths and weaknesses and to approach situations with an open and balanced perspective.

Active listening, the practice of fully concentrating on and understanding the speaker, is another key aspect of humility. By actively listening to others, we show that we value their perspectives and are open to learning from them. This practice fosters empathy and understanding, which are essential for building strong and respectful relationships.

Seeking feedback from others is also crucial for developing humility. Feedback provides valuable insights into our behaviors and how we are perceived by others. By being open to feedback, we demonstrate a willingness to learn and grow, which is a key aspect of humility. It also shows that we value the input of others and are committed to continuous improvement.

Engaging in acts of service is another powerful way to cultivate humility. Service to others shifts our focus away from ourselves and toward the needs of others. It reminds us of the importance of empathy, compassion, and generosity, and it fosters a sense of connection and community. By serving others, we develop a greater appreciation for the strengths and contributions of those around us, which is a fundamental aspect of humility.

The Impact of Humility on Society

Humility has the potential to transform not only individuals but also communities and societies. In a world that often prioritizes competition, power, and self-promotion, humility offers a different path—one that emphasizes collaboration, empathy, and mutual respect. By embracing humility, we can create a more inclusive and compassionate society where individuals are valued for their contributions and where diverse perspectives are celebrated.

In the workplace, humility can lead to more effective teamwork and collaboration. When individuals approach their work with humility, they are more likely to listen to others, value their input, and work together toward shared goals. This collaborative approach fosters a positive and inclusive work environment where everyone feels valued and empowered to contribute their best.

In communities, humility can foster a sense of connection and belonging. When individuals approach their interactions with humility, they are more likely to build strong and supportive relationships. This sense of connection strengthens the fabric of the community, creating a culture of mutual respect and support.

On a societal level, humility can contribute to social justice and equity. Humility involves recognizing the limitations of our own perspectives and being open to learning from others. This openness is essential for addressing systemic inequalities and promoting social change. By valuing diverse perspectives and experiences, we can work together to create a more just and equitable society.

The Enduring Value of Humility

Humility is a vital quality that enriches personal growth, relationships, and leadership. It involves self-awareness, vulnerability, and a genuine appreciation for others. Humble individuals are open to feedback, embrace their imperfections, and value the strengths of those around them. They approach challenges with resilience, foster deeper connections through empathy, and contribute to a culture of continuous learning.

While humility may be undervalued in a culture that often prioritizes self-promotion, it remains an essential component of a fulfilling and meaningful life. By embracing humility, individuals can create a more supportive and collaborative environment, enhance their personal growth, and build lasting relationships based on mutual respect and understanding.

Ultimately, humility is not about diminishing oneself but about recognizing our place within the larger tapestry of human experience. It is about valuing the contributions of others, embracing our own limitations, and striving for growth and improvement. In a world that often emphasizes individual achievement and self-promotion, humility offers a powerful reminder of the importance of connection, empathy, and the shared human experience. By cultivating humility in our lives, we can contribute to a more compassionate, inclusive, and just society where everyone is valued and respected for who they are.

EPILOGUE

As we draw this journey to a close, it's time to reflect on the threads of wisdom, hope, and positivity that have been woven throughout these pages. This book began with a question: *What if it's not about where we end up but about who we become on the way there?* Now, as we stand at the culmination of our exploration, it's evident that the journey itself has been rich with lessons, transformations, and moments of profound understanding.

The world we live in is often filled with noise and haste, and it's easy to get lost in the rush of daily life. We are constantly bombarded with distractions and challenges that can cloud our vision and obscure the path forward. Yet, within this chaos, there remains a quiet but powerful force—a force that is often overlooked but is always present, waiting to be tapped into. This force is positivity, and it is one of the most potent tools we have at our disposal.

Throughout this book, we have delved into the importance of positivity—not as a superficial or fleeting emotion but as a deep, abiding principle that can guide our lives. Positivity is not about ignoring the hardships or challenges that we face; rather, it is about choosing to see the potential for good in every situation. It is about recognizing that even in our darkest moments, there is always a glimmer of light to be found.

This perspective is not always easy to maintain, especially in a world that often emphasizes the negative. We are frequently reminded of what is wrong, what is lacking, and what is broken. But as we have explored through the quotes, reflections, and stories in this book, there is tremendous power in choosing to focus on what is right, what is abundant, and what is whole.

Positivity has a ripple effect. When we choose to approach life with a positive mindset, we not only transform our own experience, but we also impact those around us. A kind word, a warm smile, or a gesture of goodwill can have far-reaching consequences that we may never fully understand. These small acts of positivity are like stones dropped into a pond—their effects radiate outward, touching lives in ways we cannot predict.

In this journey, we have also explored the resilience required to maintain a positive outlook in the face of adversity. Life is filled with challenges—moments of doubt, fear, and uncertainty that can make it difficult to hold onto hope. Yet, it is in these very moments that positivity becomes most powerful. By choosing to remain hopeful and to seek out the good, even when it seems elusive, we cultivate a resilience that can carry us through the toughest times.

The stories and reflections shared in this book are not just abstract ideas—they are rooted in real experiences. They come from people who have faced life's greatest trials and have emerged stronger, wiser, and more compassionate. Their journeys remind us that positivity is not about denying reality but about embracing it with a spirit of optimism and a belief in the possibility of a better future.

As you close this book, I encourage you to take these lessons with you. Let the words and stories linger in your mind, and let them influence the way you approach your own life. Remember that positivity is not just something to be felt but something to be practiced. It is a daily choice, a habit to be cultivated, and a mindset to be nurtured.

Positivity is about more than just feeling good—it's about creating good. It's about being intentional in our actions and interactions, about choosing to uplift rather than to tear down, and about recognizing the power we have to make a difference in the world. Every day presents us with opportunities to choose positivity, to be a source of light in someone else's life, and to contribute to a world that is kinder, more compassionate, and more just. As you move forward, let these words serve one of many companions on your path.

When you face challenges, reflect on your journey for comfort and encouragement. When you feel lost or uncertain, let the wisdom shared here guide you back to the path of hope and positivity. And when you are blessed with moments of joy and clarity, use them as a reminder of the beauty that exists in the world, even in the smallest of things.

In the end, life is not just about reaching a destination but about the journey itself. It's about who we become as we navigate the twists and turns, the highs and lows, and the moments of both triumph and despair. It's about the connections we make, the love we share, and the impact we leave behind.

This book is a celebration of that journey—a reminder that no matter where you are or what you are facing, there is always a reason to hope, to dream, and to believe in the inherent goodness of life. The power of positivity lies within each of us, and it is a power that can transform not only our own lives but also the world around us.

Thank you for taking this journey with me. May the time you have spent here continue to inspire and uplift you, now and always. And may you carry the light of positivity with you, spreading it to others and creating a ripple effect of goodness, hope, and love that reaches far beyond what you can see.